NEW TESTAMENT THEOLOGY

General Editor: James D. G. Dunn,
Lightfoot Professor of Divinity, University of Durham

The theology of the Gospel of Matthew

This series provides a programmatic survey of the individual writings of the New Testament. It aims to remedy the deficiency of available published material, which has tended to concentrate on historical, textual, grammatical and literary issues at the expense of the theology, or to lose distinctive emphases of individual writings in systematised studies of 'The Theology of Paul' and the like. New Testament specialists here write at greater length than is usually possible in the introductions to commentaries or as part of other New Testament theologies, and explore the theological themes and issues of their chosen books without being tied to a commentary format, or to a thematic structure drawn from elsewhere. When complete, the series will cover all the New Testament writings, and will thus provide an attractive, and timely, range of texts around which courses can be developed.

Matthew's Gospel is the most significant Jewish–Christian document of the New Testament. For Matthew, the story of Jesus is the underlying tale of his own community, from its initial convocation by the living Jesus to its espousal of the Gentile mission following Israel's rejection. Matthew's Jesus story is as deeply rooted in his community as is the Pentateuch in Israel – hence the profoundly Jewish basis of his theology. Ulrich Luz both outlines and elucidates the contents and structure of Matthew's narrative, emphasizing its focal points: the Sermon on the Mount, the miracles, the parables, the renunciation of possessions, the Eschaton. Particular attention is drawn to Matthew's theology of judgement by works, an idea at once challenging and burdensome to Christians today and a direct outgrowth of the traumatic cleavage between the Matthean community and the Israelite majority.

THE THEOLOGY OF
THE
GOSPEL OF MATTHEW

ULRICH LUZ

Professor of New Testament Studies,
University of Bern

TRANSLATED BY
J. BRADFORD ROBINSON

CAMBRIDGE
UNIVERSITY PRESS

PUBLISHED BY THE PRESS SYNDICATE OF THE UNIVERSITY OF CAMBRIDGE
The Pitt Building, Trumpington Street, Cambridge, United Kingdom

CAMBRIDGE UNIVERSITY PRESS
The Edinburgh Building, Cambridge CB2 2RU, UK   http://www.cup.cam.ac.uk
40 West 20th Street, New York, NY 10011–4211, USA   http://www.cup.org
10 Stamford Road, Oakleigh, Melbourne 3166, Australia
Ruiz de Alarcón 13, 28014 Madrid, Spain

Originally published in German as *Die Jesusgeschichte des Matthäus*,
by Neukirchen: Neukirchener Verlag
and © Ulrich Luz 1993

First published in English by Cambridge University Press 1995 as
The theology of the Gospel of Matthew
English translation © Cambridge University Press 1995
Reprinted 1996, 1998, 2000

Printed in the United Kingdom at the University Press, Cambridge

A catalogue record for this book is available from the British Library

Library of Congress Cataloguing in Publication data
Luz, Ulrich.
[Jesusgeschichte de Matthäus. English]
The theology of the Gospel of Matthew / Ulrich Luz;
translated by J. Bradford Robinson.
p.   cm.
ISBN 0 521 43433 5 (hardback) – ISBN 0 521 43576 5 (paperback)
1. Bible. N. T. Matthew – Theology.
2. Bible. N. T. Matthew – Criticism, interpretation, etc.
I. Title.
BS2575.5.L8813   1995
226.2′06 – dc20

ISBN 0 521 43433 5 (hardback)
ISBN 0 521 43576 5 (paperback)

Contents

Editor's preface

Although the New Testament is usually taught within Departments or Schools or Faculties of Theology/Divinity/Religion, theological study of the individual New Testament writings is often minimal or at best patchy. The reasons for this are not hard to discern.

For one thing, the traditional style of studying a New Testament document is by means of straight exegesis, often verse by verse. Theological concerns jostle with interesting historical, textual, grammatical and literary issues, often at the cost of the theological. Such exegesis is usually very time-consuming, so that only one or two key writings can be treated in any depth within a crowded three-year syllabus.

For another, there is a marked lack of suitable textbooks round which courses could be developed. Commentaries are likely to lose theological comment within a mass of other detail in the same way as exegetical lectures. The section on the theology of a document in the Introduction to a commentary is often very brief and may do little more than pick out elements within the writing under a sequence of headings drawn from systematic theology. Excursuses usually deal with only one or two selected topics. Likewise larger works on New Testament Theology usually treat Paul's letters as a whole and, having devoted the great bulk of their space to Jesus, Paul and John, can spare only a few pages for others.

In consequence, there is little incentive on the part of teacher or student to engage with a particular New Testament document, and students have to be content with a general overview, at best complemented by in-depth study of (parts of) two or three New Testament writings. A serious corollary to this is the degree to which students are thereby incapacitated in the task of integrating their New Testament study with the rest of their Theology or Religion courses, since often they are capable only of drawing on the general overview or on a sequence of particular verses treated atomistically. The growing importance of a literary-critical approach to individual documents simply highlights the present deficiencies even more. Having been given little experience in handling individual New Testament writings as such at a theological level, most students are very ill-prepared to develop a properly integrated literary and theological response to particular texts. Ordinands too need more help than they currently receive from textbooks, so that their preaching from particular passages may be better informed theologically.

There is need therefore for a series to bridge the gap between too brief an introduction and too full a commentary where theological discussion is lost among too many other concerns. It is our aim to provide such a series. That is, a series where New Testament specialists are able to write at a greater length on the theology of individual writings than is usually possible in the introductions to commentaries or as part of New Testament Theologies, and to explore the theological themes and issues of these writings without being tied to a commentary format or to a thematic structure provided from elsewhere. The volumes seek both to describe each document's theology, and to engage theologically with it, noting also its canonical context and any specific influence it may have had on the history of Christian faith and life. They are directed at those who already have one or two years of full-time New Testament and theological study behind them.

University of Durham   JAMES D. G. DUNN

Author's preface

Like anyone else who wishes to write a theology of Matthew, I am faced with a fundamental decision: should I present the theology of Matthew systematically, organized by topic, as has been attempted for example by J. Ernst and R. T. France? Or should I follow the Matthean account and write a 'Matthew's Story of Jesus' in the manner of R. A. Edwards and J. D. Kingsbury?[1] I have chosen the second option, not because I am well versed in matters of literary criticism, but because I am convinced that the Gospel of Matthew is a *story* of Jesus that can only be understood when one retraces it and tries to grasp what it wished to convey to its intended readers. I have tried to interpolate several broader and more systematic sections at points in the story where it seemed most fitting to do so, just as Matthew inserted his discourses in the form of direct address from Jesus to the readers of his narrative. My own readers may decide for themselves whether this procedure is appropriate.

Hundreds of experts have written about Matthew's Gospel. The few I have mentioned in the notes (sometimes quite critically!) should know that I cited them because their writings have become especially important to me. I would like to thank them for all they have taught me. Others from whom I also learnt could not be cited; for a detailed explanation of each of my exegetical decisions I must refer the reader to the volumes of my commentary, whether completed or still in

---

[1] See J. Ernst, *Matthäus: ein theologisches Portrait* (Düsseldorf: Patmos, 1989); R. T. France, *Matthew – Evangelist and Teacher* (Exeter: Paternoster, 1989); R. A. Edwards, *Matthew's Story of Jesus* (Philadelphia: Fortress, 1985); J. D. Kingsbury, *Matthew as Story* (Philadelphia: Fortress, 1986).

preparation. But many other people also merit my gratitude. I would like to mention two in particular: Pascal Mösli, who painstakingly corrected the manuscript and compiled the index, and Isabelle Noth, who read the proofs.

This book is dedicated to Traugott Holtz, a great scholar and true friend from the former state of East Germany. During all the difficult years of socialism he never ceased to take up the cause of mankind. In the reunited country of Germany he is now among the ranks of the unemployed. It is my feeling that he (and not only he!) has been dealt an injustice. For the English edition the subchapter 'Matthew and Church History' in chapter 9 has been newly added. My German text has been translated into readable and fluent English by J. Bradford Robinson. The editor, James Dunn, has gone through the translation and made valuable suggestions. My thanks are extended to both of them for their excellent work.

Laupen, Switzerland, April 1993 ULRICH LUZ

Abbreviations

AB	*Analecta Biblica*
AThD	*Acta Theologica Danica*
BEvTh	*Beiträge zur evangelischen Theologie*
BGBE	*Beiträge zur Geschichte der biblischen Exegese*
BHTh	*Beiträge zur historischen Theologie*
BZNW	*Beihefte zur Zeitschrift für die neutestamentliche Wissenschaft*
CChr.SL	*Corpus Christianorum: Series Latina*
EKK	*Evangelisch-katholischer Kommentar zum Neuen Testament*
EThSt	*Erfurter Theologische Studien*
FRLANT	*Forschungen zur Religion und Literature des Alten und Neuen Testaments*
HThK	*Herders theologischer Kommentar zum Neuen Testament*
HThK.S	*Herders Theologischer Kommentar zum Neuen Testament, Supplementband*
ICC	*An International and Critical Commentary*
JBL	*Journal of Biblical Literature*
JSNT	*Journal for the Study of the New Testament*
JSNT.S	*Journal for the Study of the New Testament, Supplement Series*
MSSNTS	*Monograph Series, Society for New Testament Studies*
NEB	*Neue Echter Bibel*
NT.S	*Novum Testamentum, Supplements*
NTA.NF	*Neutestamentliche Abhandlungen, Neue Folge*
NTD	*Das Neue Testament Deutsch*
NTOA	*Novum Testamentum et Orbis Antiquus*
NTS	*New Testament Studies*

SBS	*Stuttgarter Bibelstudien*
TEH	*Theologische Existenz heute*
TNTC	*Tyndale New Testament Commentaries*
TRE	*Theologische Realenzyklopdie*
WA	Martin Luther, *Werke, Kritische Gesamtausgabe* (Weimar edition)
WA.DB	Martin Luther, *Werke, Kritische Gesamtausgabe* (Weimar edition: German Bible)
WMANT	*Wissenschaftliche Monographien zum Alten und Neuen Testament*
WUNT	*Wissenschaftliche Untersuchungen zum Neuen Testament*
ZAW	*Zeitschrift für die alttestamentliche Wissenschaft*
ZNW	*Zeitschrift für die neutestamentliche Wissenschaft*
ZThK	*Zeitschrift für Theologie und Kirche*

CHAPTER I

The Book

MATTHEW'S GOSPEL AS A COHERENT BOOK

Today the Gospels are very seldom read in their entirety, from beginning to end. Laypeople prefer instead to choose isolated passages for their daily Bible readings, perhaps from a book of lections. Pastors do much the same: they need excerpts from the Gospels for their sermons or instruction. Theologians often use the Gospels (and other biblical texts) as a sort of quarry or 'documentation centre', employing passages from them to substantiate one or another theological verity. This state of affairs can even be felt in Gospel research: here and there the Gospels have been described as books of pericopes or lectionaries, that is, as collections of the traditions about Jesus.[1] Hardly anything could be more incorrect than this assumption.

There are several reasons why the Gospels are only rarely read from beginning to end. One very important reason is that we know them well – or think we do. Books we know well lack the element of excitement we feel, for example, when reading a novel or short story. Instead, one prefers to read isolated passages in order to refresh the memory. But this is to overlook one very important consideration: all the Gospels, though perhaps least of all Luke's, have an internal 'line of tension' extending from beginning to end. Each has an underlying conflict that arises in the course of the narrative, reaches a climax and arrives ultimately at a resolution. In the English-

---

[1] G. W. Kilpatrick, *The Origins of the Gospel according to St Matthew* (Oxford: Clarendon, 1946), 59–100, treats Matthew's Gospel as a lectionary with a catechetical slant.

speaking world this underlying conflict is called the 'plot' of a story, though perhaps 'plan' might be a better word. The field of research known as literary criticism[2] has taken up the Gospels as a whole and contributed much of importance to their understanding.[3]

The Gospel of Matthew invites reading from beginning to end. This is made apparent by many indications in the text itself. I will begin by mentioning the so-called *signals* that frequently occur, particularly in the Prologue. By these I mean passages that stand out in context because of a fuller significance that remains unclarified when that passage is read in isolation. Why, for example, does the genealogical section list precisely four women: Tamar, Rahab, Ruth and the 'wife of Uriah', or Bathsheba? Why, in Matthew 2:3, is not only King Herod but 'the whole of Jerusalem' distraught at the news of the birth of the Messiah? What is the meaning of the quotation 'He shall be called a Nazarene' (2:23), which not even Matthew was able to trace in his Bible?[4] Why, in 3:15, does Jesus say in reference to the Baptist and himself that 'we do well to fulfil all righteousness'? Why is it so important in 4:15 that a fulfilment quotation be used to prove that Galilee is the land of the Gentiles? None of this is obvious to the reader when he or she reads the passage in question. Another passage of signal character is the section interpolated in the Parables Discourse (13:10–15), where the reader is puzzled to hear Jesus' sharp words against 'those others', suspecting that he could mean Israel. This puzzlement arises from the fact that up to now the people of Israel have actually been quite friendly toward Jesus and have listened to him in great numbers (13:1–2). Similarly, Jesus' abrupt withdrawal into the house, away from the crowd, in 13:36 comes as a surprise whose significance remains, for the moment, unclear.

---

[2] In the sense intended by the proponents of New Criticism, i.e. a close explication of the meaning of a text solely on the basis of its literary form and language.

[3] See especially Kingsbury (cf. n. 1, Preface) and D. Howell, *Matthew's Inclusive Story: a Study in the Narrative Rhetoric of the First Gospel*, JSNT.S, 42 (Sheffield: ISOT Press, 1990).

[4] See U. Luz, *Matthew 1–7* (Minneapolis and Edinburgh: Augsburg Fortress/T. & T. Clark, 1990), 132.

Related to these signals are the *prophecies* in which the Gospel abounds. One of the prophecies adopted by Matthew is the annunciation by John the Baptist of the coming of Jesus, who will 'baptize with the Holy Spirit and with fire' and 'winnow the threshing-floor with his shovel' (3:11–12). Another prophecy, this time added by Matthew himself, refers to 'those sons of the kingdom', who will be driven out, while those who 'come from the east and west' will feast with the fathers of Israel (8:11–12). Equally prophetic, of course, are Jesus' announcements of the passion, which were also known to Matthew (16:21; 17:12, 22–23; 20:18–19). Even parables may contain explicit or cryptic prophecies foreshadowing the end of the history of mankind's salvation, as happens in 21:43.

Thirdly I should mention the technique, encountered frequently in Matthew, of *key words*. Unlike their role in oral literature, they do not function as *aides-mémoire*. In a written text such as Matthew's they have a different function altogether. For example, the word 'righteousness' is highly significant in Matthew's Gospel. Its every occurrence has been added by the evangelist. Five of the seven instances of this word in the Gospel are found in the Sermon on the Mount, where it constitutes the most important key word apart from 'Father' in reference to God (of forty-five instances, twelve are in Matthew 6!). Taken together, these two words indicate the subject-matter of the Sermon. Such key words do not, of course, stand out when the Gospel is read in isolated excerpts, though they will probably strike people who read the Sermon on the Mount in its entirety. Similar key words can be found in other sections. Of twenty-five occurrences of the word 'follow', nine are in chapters 8 and 9. There is an accumulation of the word *krisis* ('judgement') in chapter 12, where five of its twelve occurrences can be found. The phrase 'Son of Man' is strewn very unevenly throughout the Gospel: there are no instances of it in chapters 1 to 7, three in chapters 8 to 10, six in chapters 11 to 13, eight in chapters 16 to 20 and eleven in chapters 24 to 26. The frequency of its occurrence in certain chapters will only strike those readers who read the Gospel as a continuous narrative. In Matthew's Gospel, key words have the same highlighting function as does underscoring today, a practice unknown in Matthew's time.

Related to key words are other forms of *repetition*.[5] Many of these were handed down to Matthew by tradition. Mark, too, in his section on the disciples (chapters 8 to 10), has three annunciations of the passion. Furthermore, many repetitions result from the fact that Matthew occasionally presents two variants of the same text, one from his Mark source and another from the 'second source' or 'sayings source' known as Q (from the German word *Quelle*, meaning 'source'). Examples of this can be found in 10:38–39 and 16:24–25, or in 12:38–40 and 16:1–4. However, since Matthew shows himself capable in many other passages of recognizing and unifying duplications it would be wrong to attribute such repetitions to literary ineptitude or mere deference to tradition. There are other repetitions for which the evangelist himself was responsible. The most famous of these is the formula 'wailing and grinding of teeth' which Matthew found in the Sayings Source (Q 13:28 = Matt. 8:12) and repeated no fewer than five times (13:42, 50; 22:13; 24:51; 25:30).[6] Other examples include the summary of Jesus' preaching and healing in 4:23 (repeated in 9:35) and his warning to the watchful disciples (24:42 and 25:13). Chapters 12 to 16 are distinguished by Jesus' various 'withdrawals' from the people. These are repeated again and again (12:15; 14:13; 15:21; 16:4), usually with the word *anachōreō*. The evangelist uses such repetitions to indicate what he finds important or to mark the divisions of a larger section. In short, his repetitions are deliberate, not proof of literary incompetence.

Similar to repetitions are *inclusions*, that is, sections bracketed at their beginning and end by a particular catchword or motif. The entire Gospel is bracketed by the fundamental Christological motif of 'God with us' (Immanuel) in 1:23 and 28:20. Inside this large-scale inclusion is another, the motif of obedience of the Son of God, which dominates both 3:13 to

---

[5] See J. C. Anderson, *Over and over and over again: Studies in Matthean Repetition* (diss., Chicago, 1985).

[6] Passages from the Sayings Source Q are indicated by references to the Gospel of Luke. Thus, Q 13:28 refers to the Q text on which Lk. 13:28 is based, whereas Lk. 13:28 refers to the Lucan text as we know it today.

4:11 and 27:38–54. One example of a shorter section 'enclosed' by identical catchwords is the central portion of the Sermon on the Mount, dealing with the fulfilment of 'the law and the prophets' (5:17; 7:12).

Of these techniques, the most difficult to recognize are the numerous *cross-references* and *flashbacks* in Matthew's Gospel. These cannot be regarded as repetitions in the strict sense of the term. Let me give a few examples. Matthew 13:12 is found in that section where Jesus speaks, somewhat cryptically, of the incomprehension of 'those others': 'For the man who has will be given more ... and the man who has not will forfeit even what he has.' The readers or listeners of his Gospel must have realized that Jesus was speaking of Israel. The verse is taken up again in 21:43 and explicated from a particular angle. There we read that 'the kingdom of God will be taken away from you'. Another good example of a cross-reference is the episode of the gravewatchers and their bribery in 27:62–66 and 28:11–15. Here the high priests and the Pharisees know that 'that impostor' once claimed he would rise from the dead after three days. The reference can only be to the passage about the sign of the prophet Jonah (12:40), where the Pharisees were also present. In other words, the 'sign' given by Jesus to his adversaries is the resurrection. Finally, I would like to refer to the very last passage in the Gospel, the so-called 'Great Commission' (28:16–20). Again it alludes to a large and wide array of earlier texts: the Immanuel motif (1:23), the temptation of Jesus on the Mount (4:8–10), the Sermon on the Mount (Matt. 5–7), Jesus' instruction to go only to the lost sheep of the house of Israel (10:5–6), the revelation of the Father and the Son to the simple at heart (11:25–27) and Jesus' announced intention to proceed to Galilee (26:32; 28:7). The final passage in the Gospel of Matthew is like a large terminal railway station in which many lines converge.

All of these literary techniques are only recognizable to readers who choose to read the Gospel as a continuous narrative rather than in excerpts and individual pericopes. Many are so difficult to recognize that they only become apparent after several readings. These are the sort of readers Matthew must have hoped for, and they must have existed in his day. Yet this presupposes a high degree of literacy among at least some members of the Matthean community. Who were the readers Matthew had in mind for his book? Perhaps they were those Christian 'sages' and 'scribes' (see 23:34; 13:52) whose task consisted in conveying 'old' and 'new' to the community. By the former Matthew may have meant the Bible, by the latter such Christian texts as his own Gospel. Whatever the case, he could not have meant the entire community, for literacy was relatively rare in the ancient world.[7] Most of the members of Matthew's community would have become acquainted with his Gospel by having it read to them.[8] Perhaps Matthew hoped for some form of public *lectio continua* for his book. Many of the literary techniques described above can also be recognized when the Gospel is read aloud from beginning to end, especially if we consider that memory in the ancient world was presumably better than it is today. Still, individual reading was preferable, as it provided an opportunity to turn back to earlier passages and thus to trace repetitions, inclusions and so forth. None the less, a lector of the Gospel could help his listeners get started by his accentuation and emphasis, and by offering an occasional explanation.[9]

MATTHEW'S PREDECESSORS

It is customarily assumed that Matthew took the Gospel of Mark as his source. He also made use of the Sayings Source or 'logia document' *Q*, a written-out but no longer extant collection of Jesus' sayings ('logia') arranged in groups by topic together with a few stories. Although it has been questioned from various angles in recent years, I consider this assumption, known as the 'two-source theory', to be correct. Still, I would like to refine it in several respects:

[7] W. V. Harris, *Ancient Literacy* (Cambridge, Mass.: Harvard University Press, 1989), 267, calculates a literacy rate of fifteen per cent for ancient Rome. The rate may have been higher among Jews, but even so one must consider that an 'ability to read' did not primarily apply to books so much as to invoices, letters and the like.

[8] In antiquity as a whole, reading was generally performed aloud rather than silently.

[9] See G. Stanton, *A Gospel for a New People* (Edinburgh: T & T Clark, 1992), 72–76.

(1) I posit the existence of various 'recensions' or critical revisions of Q. Unlike the Gospels, the Sayings Source was evidently not bound and codified but rather a loose-leaf collection of materials to which new leaves could be added.[10] These additional materials included, for example, the Beatitudes of 5:5 and 5:7–9, the saying of 6:34, and perhaps such 'logia' as Matthew 5:19, 10:5–6 and 10:23. To my mind these are relatively few; the version of Q employed by Luke may well have had a larger number of such addenda.

(2) There is a very large number of 'minor agreements' between Matthew and Luke that cannot be entirely accounted for by the two-source theory. In my opinion one must choose between two possibilities. Either Luke and Matthew employed a slightly different, presumably somewhat later recension of Mark's Gospel as we know it today (*Deuteromarkus*).[11] Or, alternatively, Luke was aware of Matthew's Gospel among the many predecessors mentioned in his Prologue (Luke 1:1) but only turned to it occasionally to settle marginal issues (perhaps because he realized it was a relatively recent work).[12] The first assumption has the drawback that it must introduce an unknown variable and can therefore in most passages be neither proved nor disproved. The drawback of the second assumption is that it scarcely explains why Luke refrained from using Matthew's Gospel in practically all truly important questions, such as that of its design, or why he excluded the Matthean special sayings. For these reasons I incline to posit the existence of a deutero-Marcan recension which departed slightly from the canonical Gospel of Mark and was available to both Matthew and Luke.

(3) Besides Mark and the Sayings Source, I feel that there is only one instance where Matthew turned to a written source: the Sermon on the Mount. Here he probably worked material

---

[10] See M. Sato, *Q und Prophetie*, WUNT, II/29 (Tübingen: Mohr, 1988), 62–68.
[11] See especially A. Ennulat, *Die Minor Agreements: ein Diskussionsbeitrag zur Erklärung einer offenen Frage des synoptischen Problems*, WUNT, II (Tübingen: Mohr, 1994).
[12] See M. Goulder, *Luke: a New Paradigm*, JSNT.S, 20/1 (Sheffield: JSNT, 1989), 22–23. Admittedly Goulder assumes that Matthew was one of Luke's principal sources.

from *Q* into a written source of the Antitheses (5:21–22, 27–28, 33–37).[13] For most of the remaining Matthean special sayings I presume that Matthew was the first to put them down in writing from oral tradition.[14]

Matthew was indebted to these sources in many ways. Apart from a few texts such as Mark 1:23–27, 4:26–29 and 12:41–44, he did not omit a single passage from his Marcan source. Even in the case of *Q* there is, I feel, only one passage (*Q* 12:49f) for which it can be argued convincingly that Matthew disregarded a Jesus saying. But most of all he was indebted to them for their substance. In many different ways they, or rather their authors, were his theological mentors.

Matthew patterned the narrative outline of his Gospel essentially on Mark. Apart from a few interpolations and the discourses he follows Mark's narrative outline very closely from chapter 12. Even in chapters 3 to 4 and 8 to 10 the Gospel of Mark served as his basic outline. None the less, he made crucial changes in the opening section of his Gospel. He created a new introduction in the narratives of Jesus' infancy in chapters 1 and 2. He inserted the Sermon on the Mount somewhat as a substitute for Mark 1:23–27. And he substantially altered the Marcan sequence in chapters 8 and 9 and greatly expanded the Mission Discourse, as he did all the Marcan discourses. Thus, one might view Matthew's Gospel as a new edition of Mark with an extended new introduction and a totally revised internal structure. It is all the more important to bear this in mind as Matthew apparently had no literature to take as his formal guide or inspiration apart from Mark's Gospel, the Sayings Source, and the Greek Bible, the Septuagint. For this reason especially, it seems to me questionable to consign Matthew's Gospel to the genre of 'biography'.[15] Matthew

---

[13] A similar view is held by S. Brooks, 'Matthew's Community: the Evidence of his Special Sayings Material', *JSNT.S*, 16 (1987), 113, who however includes 5:19 among them. Even Matthew 6:2–6 and 16–18 may have been derived from such a source.

[14] The number of redactional linguistic idiosyncracies is disproportionately large in passages such as 1:18 to 2:23, 18:23–35, 20:1–16 and 27:3–10.

[15] P. Shuler, *A Genre for the Gospels: the Biographical Character of Matthew* (Philadelphia: Fortress, 1982), thinks that Matthew wrote an 'encomium biography'.

himself probably had no notion of what a biography is. Despite certain points of similarity between his Gospel and Hellenistic or Roman biographies, we had best refer to Matthew for the moment as a 'new Gospel of Mark'. The later Church was therefore perfectly right to attach the generic label 'Gospel' to both books.

But it was not only Mark's external narrative outline that substantially guided Matthew. The two books also resemble each other in the way their narratives function. Both Mark's and Matthew's Gospels (and John's as well!) are 'inclusive stories'[16] in that the experiences of contemporary readers are included in the narrated account of the historical Jesus. Both of these Jesus stories reveal an open-endedness toward the writer's present that one might characterize with the term 'transparence'. Put differently, in both stories Jesus and his disciples on the one hand, and the readers on the other, are to a certain extent 'contemporaries'. We shall have more to say about the meaning of this later.[17]

Furthermore, a large number of basic theological ideas of Matthew's Gospel derive from Mark. I need only mention the imitation of Jesus' path of suffering, the Church as an assembly of disciples, the 'Son of David' title for Jesus the healer, the 'Son of God' title as a central Christological concept, the passion of the Son of Man, the fulfilment of scripture, and above all the openness toward the Gentile mission. Many key theological terms of the first Gospel ultimately derive from Mark, among them *akoloutheō* ('to follow' or 'to imitate'), *euangelion* ('teachings') and *kēryssō* ('to preach'). Their theological meanings will not be taken up until later. What is important here is the realization that Matthew's theology did not fall out of the blue but was considerably beholden to the Gospel of Mark.

[16] As far as I know, this expression comes from my article 'Geschichte/Geschichts-schreibung/Geschichtsphilosophie' in *TRE*, 12 (Berlin and New York: de Gruyter, 1984), 597–98, and was made into a book title by Howell in his *Matthew's Inclusive Story* (cf. n. 4). Applied to Matthew, the structure refers to what J. L. Martyn has called a 'two-level drama' in his *History and Theology in the Fourth Gospel* (New York and Evanston: Harper & Row, 1968).

[17] See pp. 62–66 below.

Matthew also owes several things to the Sayings Source. The idea of the coming judgement of the Son of Man is as central to Matthew as it was to the compilers of Q. Another important survival from the Sayings Source is Matthew's confrontation with 'this generation', meaning Israel, and with its leaders, the Pharisees and scribes. The Sayings Source also supplied Matthew with the important notion of 'little faith', which helps him to characterize the state of the disciples between faith and faint-heartedness. Above all, it seems to me that the sociological continuity between Matthew and the Sayings Source is relatively large. It is essentially distinguished by the preaching (in Q 10:2–16) of the wandering missionaries or 'early-Christian itinerant radicals', who also make an appearance in Matthew (see 10:40–42; 25:31–46). In both sources the key members of the community are prophets (Q 6:23; 11:49; Matt. 5:12; 10:41; 23:34) and teachers (Q 6:40; Matt. 13:52; 23:8, 34). The Jesus traditions in the Sayings Source, like many special traditions in Matthew's Gospel, point to a Jewish–Christian setting (see Q 16:17). As far as I can tell, the Sayings Source did not yet contain a reference to a Gentile mission.

Moreover, Matthew is rooted in the devotional observances of his community in many ways. Let me demonstrate this with one example, perhaps the clearest example of all: the Lord's Prayer (Matt. 6:9–13). This centrepiece of the Sermon on the Mount contains several of the central theological concerns of Matthew's Gospel: God is the 'Father'; his 'Will' must be followed; he grants the forgiveness that human beings in turn grant each other (see 18:23–35). The Lord's Prayer, rather than being newly formulated by Matthew, was simply retold as recited in his community. What this means, however, is that several of Matthew's central theological insights are drawn from the main prayer of Jesus and the community – the Lord's Prayer.

THE MATTHEAN COMMUNITY IN OPPOSITION TO JUDAISM

It has long been debated whether Matthew was a Gentile Christian writing for a Gentile–Christian community,[18] a Jewish Christian, or a member of a mixed community. If we decide in favour of the Jewish–Christian hypothesis, as most writers do today, we have a large number of options. The Matthean community may have abided by the Torah[19] and upheld the Law to the last 'tittle and jot', as seems to be demanded of it in 5:17–19. It may have belonged to an open-minded, cosmopolitan, Hellenistic Jewish–Christian tradition.[20] It may have belonged to a Jewish–Christian tradition still living within the association of synagogues and subject to the persecutions mentioned, for example, in 23:34–36.[21] It may have been part of a Jewish–Christian tradition that had

---

18 This is the opinion held by K. W. Clark, 'The Gentile Bias in Matthew', *JBL*, 66 (1947), 165–72; P. Nepper-Christensen, *Das Matthäusevangelium: ein judenchristliches Evangelium?*, *AThD*, 1 (Århus: Universitetsforlaget, 1958), 202–7; G. Strecker, *Der Weg der Gerechtigkeit: Untersuchungen zur Theologie des Matthäus*, *FRLANT*, 82 (Göttingen: Vandenhoeck & Ruprecht, 1962), 15–35; W. Trilling, *Das wahre Israel: Studien zur Theologie des Matthäusevangeliums*, *EThSt*, 7 (Leipzig: St Benno, 1975³), 224 [Matthew stands beyond the alternatives of Jewish–Christian and Gentile–Christian]; R. Walker, *Die Heilsgeschichte im ersten Evangelium*, *FRLANT*, 91 (Göttingen: Vandenhoeck & Ruprecht, 1967); J. Meier, *The Vision of Matthew: Christ, Church and Morality in the First Gospel* (New York: Paulist, 1979), 17–25.

19 See B. W. Bacon, *Studies in Matthew* (New York: Holt, 1930), 339–60; U. Luz, 'Die Erfüllung des Gesetzes bei Matthäus (Mt. 5,17–20)', *ZThK*, 75 (1978), 398–435.

20 See J. Gnilka, *Das Matthäusevangelium II*, *HThK*, 1/2 (Freiburg, Basel and Vienna: Herder, 1988), 533–34, and K. Stendahl, *The School of St. Matthew and its Use of the Old Testament* (Philadelphia: Fortress, 1968²), xiii–xiv. An intermediate solution is advanced by W. D. Davies and D. Allison, *The Gospel according to Saint Matthew I*, *ICC*, (Edinburgh: T & T Clark, 1988), 137–38, who set Matthew against the background of a relatively conservative Jewish–Christianity that is nevertheless receptive to the Gentile mission.

21 See Kilpatrick, *Origins* (cf. n. 1, Preface), 122; G. Bornkamm, 'End-Expectation and Church in Matthew', in G. Bornkamm, G. Barth and H. J. Held, *Tradition and Interpretation in Matthew* (Philadelphia: Westminster, 1963), 39; R. Hummel, *Die Auseinandersetzung zwischen Kirche und Judentum im Matthäusevangelium*, *BEvTh*, 33 (Munich: Kaiser, 1963), esp. 28–33; W. D. Davies, *The Setting of the Sermon on the Mount* (Cambridge: Cambridge University Press, 1966), 290–315 and 332; J. A. Overman, *Matthew's Gospel and Formative Judaism* (Minneapolis: Augsburg Fortress, 1990), 157–58; A. J. Saldarini, 'The Gospel of Matthew and the Jewish–Christian Conflict', in D. Balch, ed., *Social History of the Matthean Community* (Minneapolis: Augsburg Fortress, 1991), 38–61.

completed the breach with the synagogue, perhaps long before-hand,[22] perhaps a short while previously,[23] and had attained a new identity as part of the Great Church. There may have been tensions within it, for example between those members of the community who endorsed the Gentile mission and those who opposed it.[24]

This debate points up a particularly interesting problem. Matthew's Gospel contains sharply worded anti-Jewish passages such as 27:25, with its reference to the blood of Christ upon the people and its children. The Great Discourse of Woes on the Scribes and Pharisees in chapter 23 is so bitter and, when applied at this level of generality, so unjust that one hesitates to attribute it to a Jew. Could a Jew have condemned and railed against Jews so harshly? The anti-Jewish passages of Matthew often supplied the strongest evidence for those who argued in favour of the Gospel's Gentile–Christian origins.

The difficulty lies in the fact that quite different texts seem to be juxtaposed. After Jesus' strict injunction not to take the road to the Gentile lands or to enter a Samaritan town (10:5–6), the Gospel ends with the universal Great Commission to 'Make all *ethnē* my disciples' (28:19), where *ethnē* can mean both 'nations' and 'heathens'. Alongside a markedly Jewish–Christian Christology (in no other gospel does the title 'Son of David' play so large a role as in Matthew) we find Jesus' sharp rejection of Israel, culminating in 13:11–15 and 21:41–43. Immediately alongside instructions to abide by the Torah (5:17–19, where the Law is to be obeyed to 'the last tittle and jot') we find Jesus' Antitheses, in which he opposes his teachings to 'what was told to our forefathers', that is, to the Scriptures. No sooner had Jesus told the disciples to do everything demanded of them by the scribes and Pharisees sitting on the chair of Moses (23:2–3) than he added, at least implicitly, a massive critique of their

22 For example see H. Frankemölle, *Jahwebund und Kirche Christi*, *NTA.NF*, 10 (Münster: Aschendorf, 1974), 257–64.
23 See Luz, *Matt. I* (cf. n. 4), 67–71 and 75–76. Similar views are held by E. Schweizer, *Matthäus und seine Gemeinde*, *SBS*, 71 (Stuttgart: Katholisches Bibelwerk, 1974), 10–13 and 36–37.
24 See J. Gnilka, *Matt. II* (cf. n. 20), 531, and S. Brown, 'The Matthean Community and the Gentile Mission', *NT.S*, 22 (1980), 215–21.

teaching (23:15–24). Yet in an earlier passage he specifically warns them to be on guard against the *teaching* of the Pharisees and Sadducees (16:12). Matthew, while presupposing a knowledge of Judaism so intimate that he need not explain the Jewish hand-washing scruples, seems on the other hand often to be spreading disinformation, as when he lumps together the 'teaching of the Pharisees and Sadducees' (16:12).

This colourful *mélange* poses great demands on today's interpreters. Are our modern concepts of coherence and logic simply not applicable to Matthew?[25] Doubtless there will be great differences of opinion on this point between western European academics and an oriental Jew such as Matthew. But a thesis of this sort leaves too much unaccounted for. Either the teaching of the Pharisees is good (23:2f) or it is not (16:12). Is the one explainable as a Matthean redaction and the other as a carryover from earlier tradition?

Advocates of the Gentile–Christian origin of the Gospel of Matthew have generally solved this problem by declaring its Jewish–Christian material to be nothing more than traditional ballast. Seen in this light, Matthew was a Gentile Christian who faithfully transmitted Jewish–Christian material even when it contradicted his own thoughts. The flaw in this hypothesis is that it forces us to assume, in many cases, that Matthew handed down texts which were obsolete and of no further use to him.[26] Or do the differing statements of Jesus in Matthew's story imply that the Matthean Jesus himself turned away from Israel to the Gentiles? Did Jesus' experiences in Israel force him, in a manner of speaking, to change course? There is much in favour of this hypothesis, but it does not account for everything.

Let me now try to elaborate my own view of this matter

---

[25] To explain these tensions K. Tagawa, 'People and Community in the Gospel of Matthew', *NT.S*, 16 (1969–70), 149–62, and more recently K. C. Wong, *Interkulturelle Theologie und multikulturelle Gemeinde im Matthäusevangelium*, *NTOA*, 22 (Göttingen: Vandenhoeck & Ruprecht, 1992), emphasize Matthew's dual sociological roots in the Jewish nation and the community or, respectively, in Jewish Christianity and Gentile Christianity.

[26] This is a difficulty with the 'traces ... of the Jewish–Christian stock of ideas' that Strecker, *Weg* (cf. n. 18) has to concede to Matthew (see 34–35).

in five theses, which I shall discuss in decreasing order of certainty.

First, I am quite sure that Matthew was a Jewish Christian. His language is strongly influenced by that of the Greek Bible. Many of his favourite expressions are conditioned by contemporary Jewish usage.[27] In many cases it can be shown that traditions handed down to him originated in a Jewish–Christian setting: the additional Beatitudes in 5:7-9, the fulfilment quotations (some of which are, of course, scribal adaptations of texts handed down from Mark), and addenda such as 12:5–6, 12:11 and 24:20. A large majority of Matthew's special sayings derive from a Jewish–Christian milieu.

This is not to say that Matthew revised these traditions in a Gentile–Christian spirit. The great discussion of true purity (15:1–20) is not as radically critical of the Law in its Matthean version as in its Marcan source. In the Sermon on the Mount, the evangelist evidently wished to avoid having the traditional Antitheses mistaken as antinomian by adding Jesus' statement of intent – 'I have not come to abolish the Law and the prophets but to fulfil them' (5:17) – and the Jewish–Christian verses that follow in 5:18–19, all of which reaffirm the Law.

Second, I am firmly convinced that the Matthean community no longer remained within the association of synagogues. The evangelist repeatedly speaks of 'your' or 'their' synagogues and scribes, for example in 4:23, 7:29, 10:17, 13:54 and 23:34. There are Christian scribes living in his community (13:52; 23:34). In Matthew's Gospel the synagogue is usually burdened with negative associations (see 6:2, 5; 10:17; 13:54; 23:6, 34). This does not apply to the Temple, from which no separation had been necessary because it probably no longer existed at the time of the rift between synagogue and community. For this reason, the memories of the Temple are positive (see 5:23–24; 17:24–27; 21:13).

Third, I believe that the Matthean community lived in conformity with the Law. It goes without saying that Jesus was

---

[27] For example, *basileia tōn ouranōn, pyros* as 'status constructus', *gē* with names of countries, etc.

its foremost teacher and interpreter of the Law. It was, after all, at Jesus' bidding that the community made the two-fold commandment of love the centrepiece of the Law (22:34–40). But alongside this commandment are the 'tittles and jots' and the 'least of the Law's demands' (5:18–19). There is no reason to assume that the members of the Matthean community did not pay tithes of mint, dill and cumin (23:23). They presumably even maintained the sabbath (24:20), about which Jesus had much to teach (12:1–14). In the great discussion of purity in Mark 7:1–23 Jesus clearly rejects ritual law; in Matthew's version he does not (15:1–20). True, Matthew regards outer purity as far less important than inner purity, as represented for example by the Ten Commandments. But in his interpretation of Jesus' saying in 15:11 he no longer maintains that food which goes in by the mouth, passes the stomach and lands in the drain defiles the eater (15:17). This leads me to believe that his community upheld the Jewish purity laws without seeing anything decisive in them.

Fourth, I tend to feel that the breach between synagogue and community lay in the relatively recent past. There is much evidence to suggest that the Gospel of Matthew was written between 80 and 90 AD. Ignatius, the author of the *Didachē*, and perhaps even the author of the First Letter of Peter knew Matthew's Gospel. Luke, who probably did not know it, bears witness to a later stage of development in the transmission of the Sayings Source. Apart from the destruction of Jerusalem (22:7) there are no known references to contemporary events. Still, my main reason for suggesting an early date for the writing of Matthew is an internal one. It is much easier to explain the vehemence of the conflict with Pharisaic Judaism in his Gospel if that conflict lay in the recent past.

My fifth thesis takes up the question of the Gentile mission. Here I am least sure of myself. The Gospel ends with Jesus' instruction to minister to the Gentiles (28:16–20). This instruction had been prepared in advance by a large number of signals and announcements, for example in 2:1–12, 8:5–13, 15:21–28, 21:43 and 22:8–10. Earlier, in 10:5f, Jesus had

forbidden his disciples to proclaim the kingdom of God any-
where but in Israel. The Great Commission includes two
catchwords from 10:5–6, *poreuesthai* ('to go') and *ethnē* ('heathens'). In other words, Matthew returns to Jesus' instruction of
10:5–6 and changes or enlarges it. After Easter, he seems to be
saying, the resurrected Lord no longer sends his disciples to
Israel, or exclusively to Israel, but now to the heathens as well.
The Gentile mission is thus important to the Matthean community. The entire Gospel is designed to focus attention on it.
Up to this point everything is perfectly clear and all its interpreters are in agreement. But two questions remain:

(1) Is the Gentile mission a new task for the Matthean
community, or had it already been performing missionary
work among the Gentiles? The Gospel seems to imply that after
Easter, when the Jews and their leaders had made their
unbelief manifest by executing Jesus and rejecting the Easter
message, the Risen Lord wished to give his disciples a new
direction by sending them forth to the Gentiles. Was this the
contemporary situation of the Matthean community? Had it,
too, conducted missionary work in Israel till now, only to reach
a standstill when the rift between synagogues and communities
dashed all hopes that Israel would accept Jesus? It is not
unlikely that some Jewish–Christian communities actually did
make this decision in the days following the destruction of the
Temple. The letters of Pseudo-Clement provide further evidence that the Gentile mission began after the destruction of
Jerusalem (*Rec.* 1,64; cf. 1:41–42). For such Jewish–Christian
communities, to set out on the Gentile mission was probably
tantamount to becoming increasingly part of the Gentile–
Christian Great Church. On the other hand, judging from 24:9
and 24:14, the Gentile mission already seems to be underway in
the present (see 13:38–39). Did there already exist Jewish–
Christian groups within the Matthean community or its surroundings who had resolved to take up the Gentile mission,
and did Matthew take up their cause with his Gospel? This,
too, is possible.

(2) The second question is what sort of Gentile mission
Matthew had in mind. If Jesus fulfilled the Law and the

prophets and the Matthean community abided entirely by the Law, we can most readily imagine a Gentile mission that advocated obedience to the Law. Such a mission did in fact exist: we need only think of Paul's adversaries, the Jewish Christians in Galatia, or those Jewish Christians of whom Justin, in *Dial.* 47,2, reports that they wanted to persuade other Christians to celebrate the sabbath and submit to circumcision. There were also numerous groups who, at least in part, demanded obedience to the Law from the Gentiles: the Elchasaites, the Cerinthians and the Jewish Christians of the Pseudo-Clementines, among others. In other words, it is not impossible that the Galatian Jewish Christians who, following Paul, were later branded as false brethren and heretics were in fact Matthew's next-of-kin in the New Testament. But once again, this is only possible, not certain. The Gospel of Matthew has nothing to say about circumcision. The realities of the Gentile mission had apparently not yet left a mark on his Jesus tradition. One must also ask whether Matthew's Gospel would have established itself so quickly in the Great Church if it had been the gospel of a law-abiding Jewish–Christian sect. The Matthean community did, however, enter the larger body of the Church. We merely do not know exactly how it did so.

AN OUTLINE HISTORY OF THE MATTHEAN COMMUNITY

I shall now offer a brief sketch of the history of the Matthean community. My sketch is based on many hypotheses and reconstructions of historical tradition. It is no more than an outline of what *may* have been. Its function is to kindle the historical imagination and to elicit further outlines.

I believe that the Matthean community figured historically among those groups who sustained and cherished the collection of Jesus' sayings known as Q. This collection, the Sayings Source, presumably originated in connection with wandering Christian missionaries, prophets and teachers who travelled through the land of Israel, and with the various local communities that arose through their preaching. Perhaps the Matthean community, too, came into existence at some point

by their preaching. This thesis finds support in their common Jewish–Christian setting, their theological similarities
(especially the 'Son of Man' Christology and their common
ecclesiology), their similar church structures (prophets and
teachers), and their points of contact with the itinerant radicals
still found in the Matthean community. However, at the time
the Gospel was put down in writing the Matthean community
was no longer located in the land of Israel but in Syria. This
theory is corroborated by four pieces of evidence. First is the
mention of Syria in 4:24. Second is the curious title of
'Nazarene' in 2:23, which only makes sense if one knows that
the Syrian Christians also called themselves Nazarenes.
Another is the reference in 15:22 to the Syro-Phoenician
woman as *Chananaia*, a term less likely to be a biblicism for
'Canaanite woman' than the self-designation of the local Phoenician population. Finally, there are the early references to the
Gospel of Matthew in Syria by Ignatius of Antioch and the
author of the *Didachē*. Even so, we cannot be certain where in
Syria this community made its home; the great city of Antioch
on the Orontes is only the most probable of many hypotheses.
Nor do we know why and when the Matthean community left
the land of Israel. Was this a consequence of the Jewish War of
66 to 70 AD, which forced many Jews to abandon the country?
Or was it a consequence of the hostility and persecution intimated in the Gospel at 5:11–12, 5:44, 10:17–23 and 23:34–35?
There are no sure answers to these questions.

   In Syria, following the Jewish War and the failure of its
mission in Israel, this Jewish–Christian community of Jesus
had to find new bearings. Its members, after all, did not see
themselves as part of a new religion, called Christianity, but as
outgrowths of the nation of Israel. More than that, they saw
themselves as the core of the twelve tribes, whom Jesus had
summoned to God at the onset of God's kingdom and who were
represented in full by the twelve disciples (see 19:28). The fact
that there also existed adherents of Jesus who had long been
performing missionary work among the Gentiles, and who had
detached themselves from Israel and the Torah, doubtless
caused displeasure and opposition among many members of

the Matthean community. Special sayings such as that of the 'least of the Law's demands' (5:19) and the prohibition of the Samaritan and Gentile missions in 10:5f support this view.[28] But now the Israel mission had failed and the community found itself, unintentionally, outside the synagogues of Israel. It had encountered animosity and even, in several cases, persecution.[29] Far from being the core of Israel, the community was now excluded from Israel altogether and was forced to seek a new orientation. It was this search for a new direction in a time of crisis that the Gospel of Matthew was primarily intended to serve. To the Matthean community, for whom Jesus was the only teacher (23:8), the Gospel was an orientation on Jesus.

The discovery of the Gospel of Mark apparently played an important role in the community's reorientation. I am quite certain that Mark's Gospel, unlike the Sayings Source, did not represent the community's own traditions but entered it from the outside. Either it was a book from the Gentile–Christian Syrian communities among whom the Matthean community now lived, or it originated in the west, in Rome. Wherever it came from, it took on significance within the Matthean community. Linking his Gospel with the traditions of his own community, the author of Matthew created a new edition of the Gospel of Mark that answered the questions with which he was now confronted.

Two of the most pressing practical questions were probably that of the Gentile mission and that of obedience to the Law. Should the Matthean community, after the failure of its Israel mission, now set out on the 'road to the heathens' as many Christian communities had been doing in Syria since the days

---

[28] Both texts are generally thought to have originated in post-Easter Jewish–Christian circles.

[29] Phrases such as are found in 10:23 or 23:34 are, of course, stylizations. Floggings and executions probably occurred only sporadically (according to 23:34 among the preachers, not among ordinary members of the community), and crucifixions by the Jews not at all; see D. Hare, *The Theme of Jewish Persecution of Christians in the Gospel according to St. Matthew*, MSSNTS, 6 (Cambridge: Cambridge University Press, 1967), 19–79. In light of the final and, for the community, traumatic expulsion from Israel, these negative experiences presumably gained greatly in significance and were turned into generalizations.

of Paul? It is highly possible that the feelings and perhaps even the practices of the community differed on this point. At this juncture the author of the Gospel of Matthew now offered clear instructions in the name of the exalted Lord: 'Make all heathens (nations) my disciples' (28:19). He surely came to this realization with the aid of the Gospel of Mark, which acknowledges the Gentile mission. On the other pressing question, that of obedience to the Law, the voice of the evangelist is less forthright. Basically, he adopted a 'conservative' stance on this issue: Jesus did not abolish the Law and the prophets but fulfilled them. But he does not state what this implies for the heathens who are about to become Jesus' disciples.

Whatever the case, the decision to take up the Gentile mission marked a great step on the part of this Jewish–Christian community toward the Gentile–Christian Great Church, which at that time already existed independently of Israel. In the long term the Jewish–Christian communities in Palestine and Syria, where the Jewish populations were relatively large, now had two possibilities for the future. On the one hand, they could somehow integrate themselves into the Gentile–Christian Church, where indeed they were ultimately subsumed. This is the path which Matthew and his community in Syria set out upon, as did John the author of Revelation and his prophetic circle in Asia Minor. It is in this way that the books of these communities – the Gospel of Matthew and the Revelation of John – also came to be books of the Church. The instruction to minister to the heathens was the first step taken in this direction by Matthew and his community.

The second possibility was to form a self-contained community between Israel and the Gentile Church. Many Jewish Christians in Syria took this path. They were known to the Church Fathers from the time of Justin (*Dial.* 47,2–4) and increasingly became the object of their criticism. The point that separates them from Church Christians is their obedience to the Law; the decisive issue for Justin is whether they also wished to impose this same obedience upon the heathens. The fact that Matthew was also read in such circles is shown above all by the Gospel of the Nazarenes (presumably a sort of paraphrase of Matthew) and by the Gospel of the Ebionites. Historically Matthew stands at a parting of the ways. His fundamental affirmation of the Law is the bridge that links him with Jewish–Christianity.

CHAPTER 2

The Prologue (Matthew 1:1 – 4:22)

THE PROLOGUE AS THE BEGINNING OF THE JESUS STORY

The Gospel of Mark opens with the story of the appearance of John the Baptist and the baptism of Jesus. Matthew prefaced this opening with a genealogy (1:2–17) and an infancy narrative (1:18 – 2:23), both of which he presumably took from the oral traditions of his community. It would thus seem logical to limit the Prologue of Matthew's Gospel to chapters 1 and 2, as indeed most interpreters have done. Nevertheless, there are many good reasons for viewing the Prologue as coming to an end in chapter 4.[1] For one, 4:23 clearly marks the start of a new section; the introductory summary in 4:23 is repeated in 9:35, bracketing the intervening chapters 5 to 9 and adumbrating their contents. Conversely, 3:1 does not mark a break in the narrative; instead, Matthew leaps over a gap in narrative time of perhaps some thirty years by casually remarking 'About that time'. Verses 2:1 and 3:1 open in much the same way. Moreover, the section from 1:1 to 4:22 is self-contained in its subject-matter, even if it records two quite distinct periods of time. It is here that Matthew tells the story of the Son of God (1:18–25; 2:15; 3:13–17; 4:1–11). Fulfilment quotations of geographical import pervade the entire section (2:6, 15, 18, 23; 4:15–16). Nor should we let ourselves be misled by the nature of the source material: only today are we aware that Matthew simply prefixed chapters 1 and 2 to his Marcan source. Most of the earliest readers of his Gospel would not have known this.

[1] Following a suggestion by E. Krentz, 'The Extent of Matthew's Prologue', *JBL*, 83 (1964), 409–14.

Simply looking at the signals in the text 'synchronically' (i.e. independently of its sources) we find much more in favour of regarding the Gospel's first four chapters as its Prologue.

And what a strange prologue it is! It recounts two quite distinct episodes from the life of Jesus: his earliest infancy and his beginnings in the wilderness with John the Baptist. Between these two episodes lies a huge gap in narrative time. Matthew tells us nothing that would have most interested an ancient biographer: the youth of his hero, his upbringing and teachers, his outstanding virtues (apparent already in his childhood), his adolescence (revealing a superiority to his peers), and so forth.[2] The story of Jesus' infancy is incomplete. His birth, though prophesied at length (1:18–25), is not related so much as brushed over in a participial phrase (2:1).[3] In its place Matthew opens his story with a genealogy (1:2–17) which itself is very strange, ending in 1:16–17 with Joseph, a man who is not the natural father of Jesus at all.

In a superficial sense, then, the Prologue is the beginning of the Matthean Jesus story. In simple externals it begins just as a biography would begin, with the hero's parents and ancestors. But readers intent on hearing a biography of Jesus are puzzled from the outset. The very first text, Jesus' genealogy, takes them into a spiritual realm far removed from that of ancient biographies. As they continued reading they must have wondered at all the many things lacking in this 'biography' that should by rights have been there.

The story begins with a curious title: ' "Book of the Origins" of Jesus Christ, the Son of David, the Son of Abraham' (1:1).

---

[2] In this respect Luke 2:41–52 is a typically 'biographical' text.

[3] In popular Christian devotion the childhood of Jesus is usually recalled 'synopti-cally'. The Lucan account of Jesus' birth (Lk. 2:1–20) is inserted at Matthew 2:1, while Matthew 1:18–25 belongs between Luke 1:38 and 39. Not until Matthew 2:13 does this 'synoptic' chronology begin to show serious signs of strain: when Jesus' family flees to Egypt immediately after the departure of the three Magi, Luke 2:21–40 runs out of space. Generally a makeshift is found at this point by displacing the flight to Egypt in time. After all, Herod ordered all the innocents in Bethlehem massacred up to the age of two (2:16), thus making it easier to imagine the infant Jesus as being somewhat older on his flight to Egypt. In the Gospel of Pseudo-Matthew, for example, Jesus can already speak, calm wild beasts, ask a tall palm tree for its thirst-quenching fruit, and do much else besides.

This title is curious because one cannot tell what it actually refers to: the genealogy? the first chapter of the Gospel? the entire Prologue? the entire Gospel?[4] Among readers well versed in the Bible it kindles associations with the Greek Bible, namely with Genesis 2:4 and 5:1, where the story of the Creation is likewise called a 'book of the origins'. In other words, Matthew sets out with a new 'book of the origins', with a new *Heilsgeschichte*, or history of God's actions in the world and in mankind's salvation. It is as if he were writing the Bible anew. Yet his book does not deal with a new account of the Creation, but with the origins of Jesus Christ. The fact that he is referred to as the 'Son of David' may have been obvious to Christian readers. After all, it was widely believed that Jesus was descended from a Davidic family (see Romans 1:3). But why should he be called 'Son of Abraham'? The expression stands out because it is not an established title. Nor does it kindle associations with the Messiah: every Jew is a son of Abraham. Why is it given special emphasis here? The genealogy that follows, a genealogy beginning with Abraham, answers the question only in a formal sense. What we have here is a blank slate deliberately inserted by Matthew, to be filled in by his readers in quite different ways. His concern is that they take along in their reading an unanswered question. Not until later will they be able to say in what sense Matthew spoke of Jesus as 'the Son of Abraham'.

In the 'beginning' of the Jesus narrative that now follows, readers likewise remain under the spell of biblical stories. The annunciation of Jesus' birth (1:18–25) is reminiscent of the biblical accounts of the births of Ishmael, Isaac and Samson (Genesis 16:11, 17:19; Judges 13:3, 5). In its contents it recalls the Haggadic traditions of the birth of Moses.[5] This is all the more important as the next chapter, Matthew 2, alludes to

---

4 The last-named possibility is suggested by the word *biblos*, which in the majority of cases means a book and not part of a book. The first two possibilities, however, are supported by *genesis*, which must be read as 'origin' in light of 1:18. As this is more convincing from the standpoint of Genesis 2:4 and 5:1, I tend to view Matthew 1:1 as the title of the genealogy and its appendix in 1:18–25.

5 Amram, too, is informed in a dream by God of the future of Moses (*Jos.Ant.* 2:210ff.). According to the Haggadah he also temporarily divorces his wife.

many parallels with the Haggadic Moses in its account of Jesus' flight to Egypt:[6] Moses' birth, too, is announced to Pharaoh by magi; the child Moses is likewise threatened and rescued; the male Israelite children were similarly put to death by an evil king; Moses, too, had to flee from an evil king.

Yet the contours of the Haggadic Moses appear, in part, strangely overlapped and inverted. Events associated with the birth of Moses merge with his flight from Egypt as an adult. Egypt, formerly the land of suppression and persecution, is now a land of refuge. It is the King of Israel who now takes on the role of Pharaoh. The pagan magi, formerly members of Pharaoh's retinue, are given new roles and now pay homage to the infant Jesus as the King of Israel. In any event, readers note that Matthew is not simply retelling the Moses story in a new variant. Instead, the story of Jesus really is a new story: Jesus is at once the new Moses and the inverse of Moses. Later Gentile–Christian readers of Matthew's Gospel would also have been reminded of the childhood narratives of Cyrus, Cypselus, Zoroaster or Romulus. They too would have sensed that the hand of God must be at work with this Jesus.

In passing, our two chapters contain references and inter-ruptions that can hardly have failed to strike the reader. Especially striking, following the strange 'Son of Abraham' in the book's title, are the Old Testament quotations in 1:23 and in 2:6, 15, 18 and 23. The last-named quotation stands out especially since it concludes a section that is, strictly speaking, unnecessary. Why should the removal to Nazareth be recount-ed yet again following Jesus' return to the land of Israel (2:21)? And at the opening of chapter 3 readers must have asked, why should the story of Jesus' infancy continue in just this way, with no transition but on a completely different subject?

In short, the infancy narrative is something quite special. With its strange title, blank slates and interruptive addenda, it draws attention to the fact that it is more than merely the beginning of a story of Jesus.

---

[6] Besides this, related aspects of the legend of Abraham's birth and his imperilment by Nimrod would have been important to Jewish–Christian readers.

THE PROLOGUE AS AN ANTICIPATION OF THE JESUS
STORY: JESUS' PATH FROM THE CITY OF DAVID
TO HEATHEN GALILEE

The genealogy in Matthew 1:2–17 mentions four women: Tamar, Rahab, Ruth and Bathsheba, the latter not by her own name but by that of her husband as 'the wife of Uriah' (1:6). Once again the text gives us a signal as puzzling to readers at that time as it is to commentators today.[7] It is, however, a puzzle that can be deciphered. Why are the women named not more famous? Why not Sarah or Rebecca? What do the four women have in common so that precisely they should be mentioned?

I feel that the paraphrase of Bathsheba as the 'wife of Uriah' is an unmistakable signal. Tamar was Aramaic, Rahab a Canaanite and Ruth a Moabite. All three were non-Israelites. Bathsheba, on the other hand, was an Israelite who only became a non-Israelite through her marriage to the Hittite Uriah. This explains why she is not mentioned by her own name. Matthew, who probably inserted these four figures into the traditional genealogy, was intent on ensuring that four Gentile women appeared in Jesus' line of descent. In doing so he clearly sent a signal. The universalist perspective, the inclusion of the Gentile world, must have been important to him. Perhaps readers of his Gospel would recall the title given in 1:1 and ask whether the phrase 'Son of Abraham' is meant as a reminder that Abraham was the father not only of the Israelites but also of the Proselytes – and hence of the Gentiles.

The next story but one is that of the Three Magi, who only became 'kings' in the Middle Ages under the influence of Isaiah 60:3 and Psalm 72:10–11. This story turns on a contrast between the Magi from the east and King Herod: it is the Magi who become true worshippers of the infant King–Messiah, while Herod only pretends to worship him (2:1–12). Historically, magi were members of the Persian priestly caste. Later the

---

[7] Depending on their particular faith, exegetes either pointed to irregularities in the birth (prefiguration of the virgin birth!) or to the fact that all these women were grievous sinners (representation of grace).

term was enlarged to refer to representatives of oriental heathen wisdom, the 'intellectual elite of the pagan world'.[8] They play a positive role in our text. Jesus does not need to convert them from godless arts as they act correctly from the very beginning. They set out from the Far East, commend themselves to God's guidance, worship the infant Messiah and bring him the gifts intimated in Isaiah 60, a biblical text dealing with the Apocalyptic pilgrimage of the heathens to Zion.

Opposite them, as negative figures, are not only the present King of Israel, Herod, but the 'whole of Jerusalem' (2:3). Herod sees in the Messiah a rival to himself and tries to implicate the Magi in his evil game – with, as we shall see, well-calculated malice. But Jerusalem as a whole shudders with its semi-heathen king at the coming of the Messiah. 'All the high priests and scribes of the people'[9] become his accomplices. They help him to prepare his evil assaults through their interpretation of the Scripture. There thus arises an unholy triple alliance of evil represented by the King of Israel, his people and Israel's religious leaders. This would have surprised those readers of Matthew's Gospel who knew the actual story of Herod, for such an unholy alliance contradicts any form of historical probability. At all events, readers would have been struck by the violently worded overturning of all previous values. It is the pagan elite who now stand on the side of Jesus and act in keeping with biblical prophecies, while the elite of the holy people of Israel stand on the opposite side and begin a truly evil game against him.

The continuation in 2:13–23 shows how their game fails. God himself intervenes and reveals himself in angels and dreams. Joseph, the 'man of righteousness' (1:19), obeys, and

---

8 M. Hengel and H. Merkel, 'Die Magier aus dem Osten und die Flucht nach Ägypten (Mt. 2) im Rahmen der antiken Religionsgeschichte und der Theologie des Matthäus', in P. Hoffmann, ed., *Orientierung an Jesus: Festschrift J. Schmid* (Freiburg, Basel and Vienna: Herder, 1973), 165.

9 Matthew writes *laos* ('the sacred people'). He is fond of combining Jesus' opponents into groups of two, with the combinations being fairly arbitrary. All the Jewish leaders are opponents of Jesus, pure and simple. 'All' emphasizes the unity of the evil alliance, 'people' its representative character.

thereby becomes an instrument of the plan with which God rescues 'the child and its mother'. We are given an initial fulfilment quotation in 2:15 that reads: 'I called my son out of Egypt' (Hosea 11:1). It draws attention at once to Egypt and to Jesus' divine sonship. The heathen land of Egypt has become a place of refuge for Jesus as he flees the rage of Israel's king.

There now follows the terrible episode of the massacre of innocents in the city of David, Bethlehem. Once again we are given a fulfilment quotation – Rachel, the ancestral mother of Israel, weeping for her dead children (2:18). The fulfilment quotation imparts special significance to the massacre of the innocents. There is much more involved here than the deaths of a few guiltless children. The point is that Herod has no possible claim to be the true King of Israel. Surreptitiously and indirectly, Matthew hints that this king, and those leaders of Israel who are seeking Jesus' life, are leading Israel itself to death and perdition. In a different way, similar things will happen later in the story of the passion.

Finally Joseph returns to the land of Israel, with mother and child (2:19–21). At this point the narrative handed down to Matthew probably came to an end. Matthew, however, does not leave it at that but divides the return to Israel into two stages. Since Archelaus is ruling in Judaea,[10] Joseph travels under God's guidance to the town of Nazareth in Galilee. Matthew follows this with yet another fulfilment quotation: 'He shall be called a Nazarene' (2:23). This unidentifiable quotation taken from 'the prophets' is important to him: in the Syrian territory where Matthew wrote his Gospel, 'Nazarenes' was the name given to Christians. Jesus, the Nazarene, will therefore bear the same name as his followers, the Matthean community.

Thus Jesus grows up initially in Galilee. It is from Galilee that he goes in the next chapter to John on the River Jordan (3:13). It is to Galilee that he then returns from the wilderness (4:12). It is by the Sea of Galilee that he summons his first

---

[10] If verses 22–23 originated with the evangelist he must have had an accurate knowledge of the history of Palestine and, since he assumes a familiarity with Archelaus, presupposed that same knowledge in his readers.

disciples (4:18). In this way the catchword 'Galilee' is embedded in the minds of Matthew's readers. Before Jesus begins his actual ministry he moves once again within Galilee, from Nazareth to Capernaum, which Matthew imagined to be his place of residence (17:24–25). Just how important these geographical details were to Matthew can be seen in the fact that he appends to this move yet another fulfilment quotation: Isaiah 8:23–24, that messianic quotation in which we find the catchword 'Galilee of the heathens'. What is Matthew trying to say? For Matthew Galilee, where Jesus was to teach and preach in the synagogues and heal all the stricken among the holy people (4:23), was obviously Jewish territory. Indeed, it was virtually the heartland of Israel. Why, then, does he interpret Galilee in the light of the Bible as 'Galilee of the heathens'?

The answer is that he wished to give us a signal: the work that Jesus is about to perform in this territory will come to benefit the Gentiles. A light will appear to those living in the shadow of death. The conclusion of the Gospel, where Jesus instructs his disciples to go forth to the Gentiles, makes clear what is meant.

In this way the Prologue's geographical details are given a consistent meaning. Jesus, the Messiah of Israel and the descendant of David, born in the city of David itself, is persecuted by the King of Israel and those in power in the holy city of Jerusalem. They try to have him put to death. He flees to heathen Egypt and finally to the 'Galilee' of the heathens. It is there that Jesus, the Nazarene, summons his disciples, the 'descendants' of whom will become the Nazarenes in the neighbouring heathen country of Syria. Thus, in a manner of speaking, Jesus' path in the Prologue foretells his entire story. In that story Matthew will describe how Jesus was again persecuted by the leaders of Israel and, this time, really was put to death in the holy city of Jerusalem, and how this gave rise to a perspective of light for the Gentiles. Matthew's Prologue is thus not simply the beginning of the Jesus story; it is also, and ultimately, the narrative anticipation of that story. It foreshadows what the Gospel as a whole will relate. Readers will either sense this or, having finished the entire book, will realize it after the fact.

THE PROLOGUE AS A KEY TEXT IN CHRISTOLOGY

The annunciation to Joseph of the birth of Jesus (1:18–25) is brief and to the point. Joseph is told by the angel that his betrothed, Mary, has become pregnant through the workings of the Holy Spirit. Jesus, in other words, is the Son of God: the tradition handed down to Matthew saw the divine sonship in terms of virgin birth. Virgin birth and divine procreation are concepts remote from Judaism. According to Genesis 6:1–4 the thought that God and human beings can sexually interact is the pinnacle of sacrilege. Nonetheless, in a syncretic environment it became possible for such thoughts even to penetrate Judaism.[11] In primitive Christianity they may perhaps have been strengthened by the Christological explication given to Isaiah 7:14.[12] Matthew adopts this passage and quotes it verbatim from the Greek Bible. It keenly interested him. For Matthew, the virgin birth is an aspect of Jesus' divine sonship. It was revealed in words by God himself. Only in those two quotations that speak of Jesus' divine sonship (1:22–23 and 2:15) does Matthew add 'the Lord' to his introductory formula: 'All this happened in order to fulfil what *the Lord* declared through the prophet.'[13] Matthew adopts and takes seriously the Christology of his community, which spoke of Jesus as the son of a virgin.

Another aspect of traditional Christology was the etymological explanation given to the name of Jesus: he will save his people from their sins (1:21). Linguistically this explanation is not quite correct;[14] Matthew probably adopted it from the theology of the Greek-speaking Jewish–Christian communities. But its substance was important to him: the thought that Jesus forgives sins is echoed later in the Gospel (see 9:6) and had

---

[11] Philo seems to presuppose and to spiritualize exactly such notions in the begetting of the patriarchs; see esp. *Cher.* 40–52.
[12] Does Luke 1:31–32 also allude to this passage?   [13] See p. 37 below.
[14] Jehoshua means 'God is help'.

great repercussions on the life of the community, which received and passed on the forgiveness of sins (9:8; 18:12–35; 26:28).

Yet, for Matthew, neither the virgin birth nor the explanation of the name of Jesus is the most important aspect of Isaiah 7:14. The most important aspect is the second half of the verse: 'And his name shall be called Immanuel.' Later he translates the name Immanuel as 'God is with us'. In this way the 'birth announcement' takes on a curious form in that it gives Jesus two names, both of which are then explained. This superfluity of explanations attracts the reader's attention. Matthew found the translation of the name in Isaiah 8:8. Moreover, 'God is with us' is a basic motif that permeates all the historical books of the Bible. God accompanied Israel not only on its wanderings through the desert but also later in its history.[15] For the Matthean community Jesus meant precisely this presence of God. The final verse of the Gospel, 28:20, promises the community that Jesus will be 'with you' to the end of time. Thus, the Immanuel motif forms a bracket or inclusion around the entire Gospel of Matthew.[16] Between these two brackets it recurs again and again, explicitly in passages such as 17:17, 18:20 and 26:29, implicitly in the story of the miracles, which symbolically tell of the presence of Jesus in his community.

So important is this thought to the Christology of Matthew that we had best remain with it a while longer. Various points need to be emphasized:

(1) The category most fundamental to Matthew's Christology is derived from the Bible. It is the Bible, the story of God with the people of Israel, that gave Matthew his insight into what Jesus meant for him. In this category the biblical reminiscences that dominate the entire opening of his Gospel[17] are

[15] See W. C. van Unnik, 'Dominus vobiscum: the Background of a Liturgical Formula', in A. J. B. Higgins, ed., *New Testament Essays; Studies in Memory of T. W. Manson* (Manchester: Manchester University Press, 1959), 270–305; H. D. Preuss, '... Ich will mit dir sein!', *ZAW*, 80 (1968), 139–73.

[16] Frankemölle, *Jawebund* (cf. n. 22, ch. 1), 7–83.

[17] Note the title in 1:1, the biblical overtones in the form and contents of the genealogy, and the biblically conditioned 'birth announcement' in 1:18–25.

theologically compressed. What Matthew is about to relate, then, is a new and final account of the acts of God as given in the Bible, a continuation and supersession of the biblical story of mankind's salvation.

(2) The Immanuel motif shows that Matthew's Christology is narrative in character. The presence of God can only be related and testified, not captured in concepts. In Matthew, titular Christological categories are subordinate to narrative ones. The narrative itself is more important than a conceptual understanding of its outcome.

(3) Matthew advocates a Christology 'from above', but not in the sense later espoused by the Old Church. It is not his primary intent to define the figure of Jesus as one thing or another – for example, as God. What he does say, however, is that in the *story* of the man Jesus, God *acts*. In other words, his Christology from above is conceived from a narrative stand-point. But it remains a Christology from above in the sense that the Christological tenets most essential to the Gospel of Matthew do not revert to biblical statements about some divine emissary, such as a prophet or the royal messiah, but to God himself. For Matthew, the story of Jesus has *theological* significance. For him, Jesus is an occurrence of *God*.

(4) This Christology links the earthly Jesus (1:23) with the exalted Christ (28:20). The first mention of Immanuel at 1:23 imparts to the story of the earthly Jesus an opening toward God: in this story God is 'with' his people and his community. In this respect the story is more than 'merely' a past history of Jesus. Conversely, 28:20 links the lasting presence of the exalted Lord to the earthly Jesus: it is none other, Matthew says, than the earthly Jesus who will remain with his commu-nity every day to the end of time. In this passage, probably deliberately, he does not mention the presence of the Spirit, as does John 14:16–17 in quite similar words. In lieu of the less well-defined Spirit, which, as shown by the conflict with the false prophets in 7:15–23, had taken on a certain ambivalence, Matthew places the lasting presence of Jesus. He is the Lord of his community, which must take its bearings from him and

from his clear and forthright words.[18] This is why the 'gospel'
to be proclaimed by Jesus' disciples throughout the world is no
more than the teachings of Jesus himself, 'all that I have
commanded you' (28:20). Matthew will call this, for short, the
'gospel of the kingdom' (4:23; 9:35; 24:14). By this he meant
the teachings of the Church (*euangelion*), which consist entirely
in the proclamation of what Jesus himself had proclaimed: the
kingdom of heaven.[19]

(5) This Christology forms a backdrop to the 'transparence'
of Matthew's Jesus story, its open-endedness toward the future.
If the earthly and the exalted are one, if God is present in his
community in the form of *Jesus*, if the gospel to be proclaimed
by the community is that of *Jesus*, then clearly the story of the
earthly Jesus is already an elementary expression of the *lasting*
presence of God in his community. Thus, God will remain
continuously 'with' his community just as he did in the story of
Jesus. When members of the Matthean community read or
listened to Jesus' sayings they heard the way in which God is
'with them' *in the present*. When they listened to what Jesus said,
they heard what he is telling them today. Jesus does not, as in
Luke, belong to a past age that can never repeat itself in the
same way again. Instead, past and present, the history of Jesus
and the community's own experiences, constantly intermingle,
just as the earthly Jesus is at once the exalted Lord and vice
versa. By describing the path of the infant Jesus from the city of
David to heathen Galilee, the Prologue to Matthew not only
anticipates the path Jesus took as a whole. It equally anticipates the path taken by the community after Easter – a path
that also began in Israel, led the community into exile and
brought them to the heathen land of Syria, where they set
about ministering to the Gentiles. That which took place in the
story of Jesus was taking place anew in their own lives, and,

---

[18] See G. Bornkamm, 'Der Auferstandene und der Irdische: Mt. 28,16–20', in
E. Dinkler, ed., *Zeit und Geschichte: Festschrift R. Bultmann* (Tübingen: Mohr, 1964),
esp. 179–91.

[19] Here *basileia* is short for the basic substance of Jesus' teaching.

conversely, that which was taking place in their own present had its foundations in the story of Jesus.

These five points cover the main line of Matthew's narrative Christology. Besides this main line there are several focal points of lesser importance that illuminate sub-aspects of the story of Immanuel. I shall now turn to these focal points insofar as they appear in the Prologue.

First, we must discuss the matter of Jesus as the *Son of David*. This is the title given to him in the Gospel's heading (1:1). In the genealogy of Jesus that follows, David plays a leading role. He stands out by being referred to as 'king' (1:6). This emphasis is further underscored by the fact that the entire genealogy is divided into three groups of fourteen generations, with David appearing at the first point of division. The curious thing about the genealogy, however, is that it offers the lineage of Joseph, a man who happens in fact not to be Jesus' father. Apparently Matthew already sensed this problem, for the 'birth announcement' of Jesus that immediately follows the genealogy answers precisely the question posed by Joseph's family tree: How did the son of Mary, who was not descended from David, come to be Davidic?

The answer, given in 1:18–25, is that Joseph, at the command of the angel, refused to disown his wife. Instead, he gave her son the name Jesus and adopted him as his own child. This explains why Jesus *truly* is a son of David. The story in 1:18–25 is, to repeat a celebrated phrase coined by K. Stendahl, nothing but an 'enlarged footnote to the crucial point in the genealogy'.[20] Jesus is thus a son of David in exactly the sense required by Judaic messianology: he is a physical descendant of David's family. For this reason, too, verses 1:18–25 belong to the 'Book of the Origins' of Jesus (1:1). In later passages Matthew will stress Jesus' Davidic lineage in new and different ways. For the time being, however, he adopts the Judaic conception of the Son of David and engages his Jewish–Christian readers at the point where their own Christological

[20] K. Stendahl, 'Quis et unde? An Analysis of Matthew 1–2', in W. Eltester, ed., *Judentum – Urchristentum – Kirche: Festschrift J. Jeremias*, *BZNW*, 26 (Berlin: Töpelmann, 1964²), 102.

ideas have placed them. Jesus, then, is truly the Messiah of Israel.

Immediately thereafter Jesus is spoken of as being the *Son of God*. Here, too, Matthew engages his readers at the level of *their* Christology. Jesus is born of the Spirit, the son of a virgin. This testifies to his divine sonship. This latter is important to Matthew, and he clearly underscores it once again in 2:15 with a fulfilment quotation: 'I called my son out of Egypt.' Just how important Jesus' divine sonship is to Matthew is again emphasized in 1:22, where God himself is cited as the author of the quotation. Exactly what 'Son of God' meant to Matthew himself remains shrouded in mystery. He merely intimated, with the two fulfilment quotations, *that* this expression is important to him. Readers must therefore wait for an explanation, and they are given it, in short order, in chapters 3 and 4 of his Gospel.

The next passage at which this expression occurs is in the story of Jesus' baptism (3:17). Once again it is God who reveals Jesus as his son. New to Matthew, however, is another consideration expressed in verses 14–15: John, the lesser of the two, refuses to baptize the greater man, Jesus, although Matthew's readers have long been aware that he is the Son of God.[21] Jesus, it need hardly be mentioned, does not stand in need of atonement! His answer – indeed, his first words spoken in the Gospel of Matthew – are as follows: 'We do well to fulfil all righteousness' (3:15).

John and Jesus thus both fulfil the stipulations of 'righteousness', God's will as commanded of his people.[22] John does

---

[21] Diachronically because they are already aware of the story of the baptism given in Mark 1:9–11, synchronically because they have just read the story in Matthew 1:18–25 and 2:15.

[22] *Dikaiosynē* is, above all, a key concept in the Sermon on the Mount. In Matthew's Gospel the word occurs exclusively in redactional contexts. It is debated whether the word means, at every occurrence, the demands of God to be fulfilled by man (this is clearly its meaning in 3:15; 5:10, 20; 6:1; 21:32) or the righteousness promised or granted to man by God in the Pauline sense (as is possibly, but not necessarily, its meaning in 5:6 and 6:33). Interpreting the relatively few ambiguous occurrences on the basis of the unambiguous ones, I assume that in Matthew *dikaiosynē* always refers to the righteousness demanded by God and required of man's actions.

so by baptizing Jesus, Jesus by humbly submitting to baptism. In this way the Matthean community comes to learn why the lesser man baptizes the greater. It is precisely in reference to this deed of righteousness that the voice of God now resounds, directed not at Jesus (as in Mark 1:11) but at the assembled people and the listening community, formulated in the third person: this, the man who consistently obeys God's will, is the Son of God.

Matthew, then, links Jesus' divine sonship with his obedience. This lineage has a 'vertical' component: God alone can reveal the secret of Jesus' divine lineage (see 11:25–27; 16:17; 17:5). But it also has a 'horizontal' component: the Son of God is the just man who is fully and representatively obedient to God's will. In terms of tradition, this implies that Matthew drew not only on the messianic conception of divine sonship (as appears, say, in Psalm 2) but also on the conception found in the texts of the suffering righteous, above all in Wisdom of Solomon 2.[23]

The passage that follows in 4:1–11, regarding the temptation of Jesus, expresses the same thought. Here Jesus demonstrates his divine sonship (4:3, 6) not by working miracles or seizing power as a secular ruler, but by appealing to and obeying God's word. Later this thought will recur in a quite similar manner in the story of the passion. The Son of God is the man who, resisting the temptation of the scribes to save his life, refuses to descend from the cross and drinks the cup of suffering that God has offered him. The story of the Crucifixion (27:38–54) is thus another section in which Matthew expounds his understanding of the obedient Son of God in compressed form. We might even be tempted to speak of a second large-scale inclusion in the Gospel of Matthew. After the notion of 'God is with us' has formed the outer brackets (1:23; 28:20), an inner bracket is added dealing with the obedience of the Son of God (3:13 – 4:11; 27:38–54). The same thought recurs in the middle of the Gospel. Once Peter has acknowledged the Son of God (16:16–17), Jesus points the disciples to the path of obedi-

---

[23] Wisd. of Sol. 2:13–18 is alluded to in 27:40–43.

ence, which is that of suffering (16:21ff.).[24] It is precisely here that they encounter failure.

As the Matthean story of Jesus will later show, God is present precisely by being with his obedient Son, whose path leads to suffering and death. He who, on the mountain, rejected the devil's offer of world domination (4:8–10) and chose the path of obedience, will for this very reason, again on a mountain, be granted all the power in heaven and on earth at the end of his chosen path of obedience (28:16–20).

THE FULFILMENT OF THE SCRIPTURE

The Prologue contains five biblical quotations introduced by the stereotyped formula 'This was to fulfil the words spoken through the prophet' (1:22; 2:15, 17, 23; 4:14). In the Gospel of Matthew there are several more quotations with this 'fulfilment formula', sometimes slightly varied as necessary: 8:17; 12:17–21; 13:35; 21:4–5; 27:9–10. Quite similar formulae introduce the quotations in 2:6 and 3:3 as well as, outside the Prologue, 13:14–16 and 24:15. Most of these quotations (e.g. 8:17; 12:18–21; 13:14–16; 21:5) are found in special sayings or have been inserted into the Marcan text. Thus, as explicit quotations, they originated with the evangelist himself, even if in some cases the relevant biblical text had already exercised an influence on the source traditions in question.[25] Researchers are fairly in agreement that the stereotyped introductory formula originated with the evangelist Matthew. It provides important insight into his understanding of Scripture. Presumably he was inspired by Mark 14:49 to coin this unusual turn of phrase on the 'fulfilment' of the Scripture. Doubtless the language of the Bible influenced him as well. The closest parallel is found in 2 Chronicles 36:21, though it is unlikely that Matthew consciously drew on this passage.

A large number of fulfilment quotations are noteworthy for their striking wording. The evangelist himself seems to have

---

[24] Note the reminiscence of 4:10 in 16:23 (*hypage ... Satana*).
[25] As is certainly the case in Isaiah 6:9–10 (see Mark 4:12 par.) and perhaps Zechariah 9:9 (see Mark 11:2ff.).

been familiar with the Greek Bible (Septuagint). In many cases where he includes a quotation or allusion from his sources, Mark or *Q*, his wording has been slightly adapted to conform with the Septuagint. This leads us to conclude that the evangelist was familiar with the Septuagint but did not have any biblical scrolls at hand while writing out his Gospel – with the possible exception of Isaiah.[26] Most of the fulfilment quotations, apart from 1:23, 3:3 and 13:14–16, are quite remote from the wording of the Septuagint, revealing instead many an influence from the Masoretic text or from Targums, the name given to Aramaic translations or paraphrases from the Old Testament.

These findings can be interpreted in either of two ways. The first hypothesis assumes that these quotations, with their peculiar wordings, are basically pre-Matthean, deriving for example from a pre-Matthean collection of Scriptures ('testimonies') or the work of a scribal school. According to the other hypothesis, Matthew himself was responsible for these peculiar wordings. In this case Matthew was a sort of 'Targumist' who altered and shaped the wording of the biblical texts to suit his interpretation, as did, for example, the biblical exegetes of the Dead Sea Scrolls and, occasionally, Paul.[27] To my mind these two hypotheses are not mutually exclusive: Matthew may have adopted biblical quotations in a peculiar wording *and* revised them. I assume that Matthew's revision of the wording in the quotations was relatively slight. In any event, this seems to be the case with those quotations he took from the Gospel of Mark or from the Sayings Source. And there is no compelling reason why he should have *specially* singled out a particular group of quotations for revision.

Besides, only to a relatively small extent can the wordings of the quotations be explained on the basis of Matthew's interpretative biases. I assume that Matthew owes a number of his biblical quotations to Christian scribes. Since many of these quotations can be used practically only in their present con-

---

[26] See Luz, *Matt. I* (cf. n. 4, ch. 1), 135.

[27] See D.-A. Koch, *Die Schrift als Zeuge des Evangeliums*, *BHTh*, 69 (Tübingen: Mohr, 1986), 102–98.

text,[28] these scribes must have transmitted and revised the relevant Jesus tradition or the Gospel of Mark. Matthew himself was therefore, in my opinion, not a scribe, but stood in close contact with scribes in his community.

If Matthew did not revise a particular group of quotations from the prophets to suit his exegetical ends, the question naturally arises why he emphasized this group of quotations with a special introductory turn of phrase, the 'fulfilment formula'. The answer may be quite simple: he inserted the fulfilment formula as often as possible. Of course he could not insert it everywhere, but only where the story of Jesus really did involve the fulfilment of a prophecy. He did not insert it where there was no explicit quotation from the Scripture. Nor did he generally use it in those passages where Jesus himself argues on the basis of the Bible[29] or addresses his listeners with words taken from the Bible. These aside, one must conclude that Matthew inserted the fulfilment formula almost everywhere it fitted. In other words, it is not important for his understanding of a particular group of quotations from the prophets, but for his understanding of the prophets *per se*. Fulfilment quotations are especially numerous in the Prologue. Here, at the beginning of his Gospel, the evangelist wished to familiarize his readers with his view of the prophets. What was that view?

I think that two aspects were important to Matthew. First, it was important that the words of the prophets be fulfilled in the man Jesus and in his story. In other words, the story of Jesus was, for Matthew, an age of fulfilment, ordained and singled out by God, much as was the age of the Teacher of Righteousness and the foundation of their own sect for the Essenes in Qumran. Second, the reiteration of the fulfilment formula is intended to announce Matthew's programmatic claims to the witness of the prophets: it is in Jesus, and in none other but him, that their prophecies are fulfilled. In 5:17, in much the

---

[28] For example, Hosea 11:1 = 2:15 must have been discovered and handed down in connection with the flight to Egypt, Zechariah 9:9 = 21:5 with the entrance to Jerusalem, and Zechariah 11:13 = 27:9 with the death of Judas.

[29] Except in the modified introductory phrase 13:14.

same spirit, Matthew applies the word 'fulfil' programmatically to the 'ethical' portions of the Bible, the commandments of the Law and the prophets, saying that Jesus has come to fulfil them. Matthew lived at a time when the bonds connecting his community with Israel's synagogues had been severed. His community did not view itself as a new 'Christian' congregation but as the true core of the nation of Israel, summoned by Jesus to God. This led him to reformulate, in a programmatic spirit, Mark's incidental Christian notion of the fulfilment of Scripture. Given the rift between those parts of Israel that believed in Jesus and those that did not, the Scripture could only become an object of contention. The Christian communities raised claims to the legacy of Israel just as did the synagogues of the Pharisees.

In Judaism at that time, the only way to interpret the words of the Scripture was as a living and currently valid utterance from the standpoint of the present. The initiators of this debate over the Bible were incapable of distinguishing between the witness of the Scripture and *their* interpretation of that witness. To put it another way, there was, for them, no such thing as a witness of the Scripture apart from their own interpretation. Seen in this light, Matthew is one of the earliest witnesses in an unfortunate conflict over the Scripture that burdened relations between Christians and Jews with endless disputes up to the time of the Enlightenment. There was no way of settling these disputes so long as there was no way to read the Bible apart from a Christian or Jewish confessional standpoint. Thus, at any given time, the party that proved to be the more powerful for other reasons – such as political ones – claimed and exploited the victory for itself. Not until the Age of the Enlightenment, with its distinction between the meaning and the significance of a text, did this situation change. Only then did a discussion of the Bible become possible between Jews and Christians.

Returning to Matthew's fulfilment quotations, part of this discussion involves a concession on the part of Christians that, in most cases, the original meaning of the biblical passages cited by Matthew is very remote from their Christian interpretation. In other words, the thought that God was keeping his promises in his dealings with the historical Jesus – a thought of great importance to Matthew and the primitive Church, since without it Jesus would have been unintelligible as the Christ – is at the same time a very precarious one. Perhaps it is more akin to a postulate of faith than an item of historical knowledge. It says more, perhaps, about the Christian understanding of history than about history itself.

CHAPTER 3

The discourse on the Mount (Matthew 5 – 7)

In an introductory summary Matthew had reported that Jesus went about the whole of Galilee, 'teaching in the synagogues, preaching the gospel of the kingdom, and curing whatever illness or infirmity there was among the people' (4:23 = 9:35). Now, at the opening of his story of Jesus, he will relate how Jesus taught (chapters 5–7) and healed (chapters 8–9). His doctrine, the 'gospel of the kingdom', is contained in the Sermon on the Mount. Especially over the last two decades the Sermon on the Mount has become a central text, exercising a fascination far beyond denominational boundaries. Even today it kindles longing and hope for a new breed of human-kind and a better world.

FOR WHOM IS THE SERMON ON THE MOUNT INTENDED?[1]

Is the Sermon on the Mount a new ethic for the world? Or is it an ethic solely for the community, intended to be practised by Christians alone and not, as Martin Luther maintained long ago, by persons holding secular office?[2]

One clue is likely to be found in the backdrop against which Matthew set the Sermon on the Mount. Jesus climbs to the top of the mountain 'when he saw the crowds' (5:1). Why? To escape them, or the better to be understood by them? The disciples gather round him; apparently what he is about to

---

[1] The title of this section is taken from the important book by G. Lohfink, *Wem gilt die Bergpredigt?* (Freiburg, Basel and Vienna: Herder, 1988).
[2] The classical text is M. Luther, 'Von weltlicher Obrigkeit, wieweit man ihr Gehorsam schuldig sei' [1523], *WA*, 11, 245–80.

teach is intended for them (5:2). But the crowds listen as well. At the end of the Sermon Matthew consciously adopts turns of phrase from Mark 1:22 and writes: 'The people were astounded at his teaching, for unlike their own teachers he taught with authority' (7:28).

Viewed diagrammatically, this conjures up the image of a double circle of listeners, with the disciples gathered round Jesus and the people some distance apart. The end of the Gospel shows that Matthew did not word this accidentally or haphazardly: it is the disciples who are told to transmit to the Gentiles 'all that I have commanded you' (28:20). These final words refer primarily to the Sermon on the Mount. The Sermon, then, is the heart of the Great Commission to teach the Gentiles. In this respect it is precisely *not* intended to be limited to the inside of the Church. Nonetheless, the first recipients of the Sermon are the disciples. Matthew puts special emphasis on them, but not because the Sermon on the Mount applies to them alone and is meant to be realized within the confines of a closed community. Nor does he emphasize them solely because they alone are to propagate Jesus' commandments in the world. Rather, he does so because they are the first persons to enact the Sermon. In Matthew's view, missionary work consists not least in having men praise God for the good deeds of the disciples (5:16). Their righteousness is meant to be superior, and not only to that of the scribes and Pharisees (see 5:20). Later we shall return to this ecclesiology of the 'Church obedient'.[3] The Sermon on the Mount is an ethic for the disciples only insofar as, for Matthew, the sole difference between disciples and non-disciples that matters is the difference in their deeds. On the Day of Judgement the tree will be judged by its fruit (7:17–19).

The Sermon on the Mount is not the internal ethic of a sect whose members behave differently toward the inside and the outside worlds. This much is clear from the Sermon's contents. I shall give only a few examples. Very rarely do the verses of the Sermon on the Mount presuppose the special conditions of

---

[3] See pp. 75–80, 89–91 and 129–132 below.

the Matthean community.[4] The Lord's Prayer, in particular, is a prayer for the whole of humanity, not one that deals with situations typical of the disciples. Similarly, the enclosing admonitions in 6:2–18 do not contrast the behaviour of hypocrites in, say, the synagogues, with that of another community at a different place of worship.[5] The Antitheses in 5:21–48 take up the Ten Commandments, the fundamental ordering principle of the life of the entire nation of Israel. The Golden Rule that concludes the main section of the Sermon in 7:12 generalizes the Commandments and elevates them to a universal plane. It unites 'the Law and the prophets', the very foundations of Israel, into a principle of behaviour that is universal and intelligible to all. The concluding section in 7:13–27 opens with the admonition of the two ways, an ethical maxim belonging both to the Greeks and the Jews. Matthew is well aware that his community, too, needs this admonition.

The upshot of all the foregoing is something quite important. The Sermon on the Mount is, for Matthew, not a speech of the sort that might have been written down by a Greek historian. It is not intended to describe 'the way things were', what the great religious prophet Jesus probably said to his disciples and the Galilean crowds at the beginning of his public ministry. Rather, the main thrust of the Sermon on the Mount is Jesus' preaching as it applies to the present. It supplies the contents of the mission to be proclaimed to the world by the community, and the guiding principle by which that community is to measure its own works. The Sermon does not recount an episode from the historical past, like the speech of a grand statesman in a book of ancient history. Instead, it is 'spoken to the winds', directly addressing its present-day readers. In this respect it resembles the Pentateuch. Similarly, in Deuteronomy Moses speaks directly from Sinai to the Israelites of the eighth or seventh century BC, his words leaping over the gap of the

---

[4] As happens for example in 5:10–16, in the teaching on worry directed to the wandering radicals (6:25–34), and in the conflict with the false prophets (7:15–16, 20–23).

[5] The German term *Kultdidachē* ('instructions regarding cultic worship') frequently applied to 6:2–18 is very misleading.

centuries. In the Matthean Sermon on the Mount, whose situation recalls Exodus 19 and 34, Jesus does exactly the same thing: he speaks 'to the winds', expressing things intended for Matthew's readers. Like all the Matthean discourses, the Sermon on the Mount is more than simply part of Matthew's narrative thread; it is also a direct address to his readers. In this way it is in agreement with Matthean Christology, for the historical Jesus, whose story Matthew relates, is at the same time the present Lord, speaking to the community in its own present time.

THE STRUCTURE OF THE SERMON ON THE MOUNT

Two further basic questions regarding the Sermon on the Mount deserve mention as they dominate current discussions of this subject. The first is the question of its *fulfilability*. Is the Sermon on the Mount, especially the central demands contained in the Antitheses, capable of being fulfilled, or is it so remote from reality that human beings are destined to falter? Oddly, this question was almost never asked by the Old Church. The answer given ever since the High Middle Ages is that some of its demands were meant to be understood as 'evangelical counsels' (*consilia evangelica*). Rather than being directed at all Christians they figured as guidelines to be followed by clergymen and monks.[6] The theologians of the Reformation made a distinction between the 'two realms' of community and world. In the worldly realm, Christians who exercised an 'office' as politicians, parents, soldiers or merchants were given dispensation not to live in accordance with the Sermon, but were obligated to have love function indirectly as the measure of their lives. As there is scarcely an area in life in which Christians do not have an 'office' – all of us, after all, live within a family, economy or state – this interpretation caused the Sermon to be interiorized. It became

---

[6] It should be said, however, that this is not the typical Roman Catholic interpretation of the Sermon on the Mount. It is a reading influenced by Matthew 10 and 19:16ff. that did not explicitly enter the exegesis of the Sermon until the High Middle Ages, especially in the writings of Rupert von Deutz.

the quintessence of Christian piety, or showed mankind the true nature of God's will, thereby making men and women aware of their sinfulness. Behind all these efforts lay a firm belief that the Sermon on the Mount cannot be fulfilled if taken literally. In one way or another they express a breach with or capitulation in the face of God's will, quite often even ethical schizophrenia. In today's discussions of the Sermon on the Mount its non-fulfilability and absoluteness are criticised not least by Jews. In the course of their history they have experienced often enough that Christians do not, in fact, love their enemies and will not forgo the use of violence.[7]

The other question regarding the Sermon on the Mount is that of *mercy*. It is bound up with the realization that the Sermon poses excessive demands on mankind and, at the same time, points up the Protestant critique of those excesses. Is the Sermon on the Mount devoid of grace and mercy, seemingly asking the impossible of men and women and yet subjecting them at the end of time to the Last Judgement? Faced with the Sermon on the Mount, are we not forced to admit that our house is built on sand? What has become of Paul's notion that mankind is justified through *grace* alone?

This question has been sharpened by recent discoveries in redaction criticism. It was discovered, for example, that the Matthean Beatitudes in 5:3–10, unlike the original Jesuanic Beatitudes, shift the emphasis away from the comfort of salvation for those in dire and inescapable need. Jesus' principal object was to proclaim that the kingdom of God, paradoxically and surprisingly, belongs to those who are poor, who weep and suffer hunger (see Luke 6:20–21). Matthew has altered this emphasis: the poor have become the 'poor in spirit', the hungry have become those who 'hunger and thirst for righteousness'. Their ranks have been joined by the non-violent, the peacemakers, the merciful, and so on (see Matthew 5:7–9). In particular, exegetes debate how far the emphasis has been

---

[7] J. Klausner, in *Jesus von Nazareth* (Jerusalem: Jewish Publishing House, 1952), 547, asks with justification: 'Did, for example, Jesus himself remain true to his doctrine? Did he love the Pharisees, who were merely his theoretical opponents and not even his true enemies?'

shifted toward the ethical. They ask whether the phrase 'poor in spirit' really does mean the humble, as was later maintained by the Old Church, or whether 'hunger and thirst for right-eousness' also connotes an active involvement on behalf of righteousness. But no matter how these isolated problems are decided, the shift of emphasis in Matthew is undeniable: men and women are blessed for the sake of a particular stance, or even a particular action. This tenor permeates the entire Sermon on the Mount. The 'light of the world' – as the disciples are called – consists in their good deeds, which shine in the world so that mankind will give praise to the Father (5:14–16). Does Matthew mean that those persons are blessed who strive to make their righteousness superior to that of the Pharisees and scribes? And are those condemned whose 'fruits' – meaning their deeds – are deemed insignificant or slothful by the Son of Man at the end of time (see 7:15–23)? Is Matthew the classical exponent of a non-Pauline righteousness of works?

One possible response to these unsettling questions is the Protestant thesis that the purpose of the Sermon on the Mount lay principally in making human beings conscious of their sinfulness.[8] In the language of church dogmatics the Sermon would then belong to what is called *usus elenchticus legis* – the application of law to disclose sin. Another response are the many exegetical attempts to reinterpret the Sermon on the Mount in Pauline terms. Such attempts are still being made today.[9]

An initial answer to these questions is provided by the Sermon's *structure*. Matthew positioned it very carefully in his Gospel.[10] It is part of his Jesus narrative, the story of Imma-

---

[8] Definitively discussed in E. Thurneysen, *Die Bergpredigt*, *TEH*, 105 (Munich: Kaiser, 1965).

[9] A very impressive example of this sort of interpretation is, in many ways, H. Weder, *Die 'Rede der Reden'* (Zurich: Theologischer Verlag, 1985).

[10] The Sermon on the Mount is embedded in the Gospel of Matthew within several inclusions: 5:2 / 7:29, 5:1 / 8:1, 4:25 / 8:1, 4:24 / 8:16, 4:23 / 9:35, 4:18–22 / 10:1–4 and 4:17 / 10:7. The same principle of inclusion continues within the Sermon itself. This fact, and the similarity of its redactional vocabulary with the rest of the Gospel, prevent me from agreeing with Betz that the entire Sermon is of pre-Matthean origin. See H. D. Betz, 'The Sermon on the Mount in Matthew's Interpretation', in

nuel, of the presence of God 'with us'. It is not accidental but intentional that the evangelist incorporates these ethical proclamations into a story of God's actions with his people, just as, in the Pentateuch, the appearance of the Deity on Mount Sinai is incorporated into the story of God leading his people out of Egypt. From chapters 1 and 2 onward Matthew wrote a new story of a new Moses. The ascent of and descent from the mountain in 5:1 and 8:1 are doubtless meant to recall Exodus 19 and 34.[11] Thus God's will, as proclaimed in the Sermon on the Mount, is not simply an abstract command; it is the command of that same God who accompanies his people in the form of Jesus. Matthew, or rather Jesus, explicitly states that it is a command from the Father.

In its structure, the Sermon on the Mount itself is a literary work of art. It is bracketed by a selection from the Sayings Source, the Sermon on the Plain (*Q* 6:20–49). For the Antitheses, and perhaps also for 6:2–18, Matthew possessed another written source into which he collated additional material from *Q*, including passages from the Sermon on the Plain (*Q* 6:27–36). He has expanded his written sources with added material from *Q*, excerpted from various parts of that source and woven into the fabric at topically related locations. There are very few special sayings (5:14; 7:6). Many texts have been heavily subjected to redactional revision (e.g. 5:6, 13, 16–19, 48; 7:12–14, 21–23); relatively few are entirely redactional (5:10, 17 [?], 20, 31, 38, 43; 6:1; 7:15, 19–20). The final result of this quite mechanical and traditionalist redaction is a literary miracle of symmetry, poise and unity.

The Sermon on the Mount falls into three sections: a preamble (5:3–16), a main section (5:17 – 7:12) and a conclusion (7:13–27). The main section is in turn divided into three sections (Matthew was very fond of tripartite divisions): the Antitheses (5:21–48, with introduction in 5:17–20), the central

---

B. Pearson, ed., *The Future of Early Christianity: Essays in Honor of H. Köster* (Minneapolis: Augsburg Fortress, 1991), 259–66.

[11] I do not feel, as do Davies and Allison, *Gospel* (cf. n. 20, ch. 1), 427, that Matthew 1 to 5 can be conceived as a large-scale parallel to the Book of Exodus. However, there is no denying *that* these chapters contain references to that book.

text (6:1–18) and an epilogue (6:19 – 7:11, with summation in 7:12). Verses 5:17 and 7:12, containing the idea of the fulfilment of the Law and the prophets, form a bracket around the central section. Exactly in the middle of the Sermon is the Lord's Prayer (6:9–13). It is flanked by sections dealing with devotional observances and, especially, the Law – in short, with the relation of mankind to the heavenly Father. The word 'Father' dominates this central section, occurring no fewer than ten times. The question of 'outward' righteousness – what must I do? – is taken up in the Antitheses. They are immediately followed by a section dealing with mankind's relation to God, that is, with the 'inward', religious dimension of righteousness. The practice of righteousness then leads to prayer, a prayer directed toward a Father who always knows and hears the pleas of his children (6:7–8) because he can see into their secrets (6:4, 6, 18). The epilogue, from 6:19 to 7:11, is similarly structured. It opens with a topic of 'superior righteousness' that is of crucial importance to Matthew – the relation of Jesus' disciples to worldly possessions (6:19–34) – only to end once again in prayer, to the Father who answers the pleas of his children (7:7–11).

It is, therefore, impossible to reduce the Sermon on the Mount to its ethical core – the Antitheses – and to act as if an understanding of them alone suffices for an understanding of the entire Sermon. Rather, the problem is to interpret the Sermon as a holistic entity. The entire Sermon on the Mount is a proclamation of the will of God to men and women who are children, and who are permitted to pray to their Father because he is near to them and hears them. The Sermon is not simply a promise of salvation, nor does it merely pose demands. Instead, it represents a continuing relation, confronting those men and women with whom God is prepared to walk with the demands he imposes upon them. At the same time, precisely because of those demands, it leads them to a sense of promise from that very God who dwells among human beings before they dwell with him. One might say that the Sermon on the Mount is primarily concerned with the prayer of active men and women, or that its central thrust is the justification by

grace alone of those who strive for righteousness. Such paraphrases may puzzle people who have been trained to think in
terms of the Protestant theology of justification. However, they
will be familiar to those who proceed from Jewish thought. To
Jews, God's Law is his greatest gift to his people.

Something similar is reflected in Matthew's understanding
of the Lord's Prayer (6:9–13). I do not feel that the evangelist
has altered the wording of this prayer; he probably inserted it
in his Gospel as it was spoken in his community. The important
thing to note is that the Lord's Prayer is, to a high degree, the
prayer of active men and women, a prayer that includes the
actions of human beings and virtually makes those actions its
contents. Without mankind's obedience to the will of God it is
no more conceivable that his 'will be done' than that his 'name
be hallowed'. The plea for forgiveness – 'as we forgive those
who have wronged us' – even incorporates human action
explicitly into the prayer. The way Matthew imagines this to
happen is elucidated in the parable of the unmerciful debtor
(18:23–35). The plea for forgiveness similarly encompasses
mankind's responsibility; it is theological hair-splitting to focus
the debate on whether God himself created the temptations of
mankind and must thus be held accountable for them. The
Lord's Prayer is a prayer of active and obedient men and
women, not of those who let their hands rest in their laps and
direct their gaze humbly upward. Matthew's main concern is
not only that 'Need teaches to pray' – although this is also
congruent with his thought (see 8:25!) – but equally that
'Action teaches to pray'.

Our reflections on the structure of the Sermon on the
Mount, and particularly of its central section, 6:1–18, offer
clues to the question posed at the outset of this sub-chapter.
Mercy and obedience, promise and demand – all are inter-
linked in Matthew. The will of God is the will of the Father; his
demand is the demand of him who is with us. The question of
the Sermon's fulfilability also shows signs of receiving an
answer. Human beings are not left to their own devices in their
striving for superior righteousness and perfection. They are
sustained by God. They are permitted to pray. At least in this

respect Jesus' command is an 'easy yoke' (see 11:30). But this clue is not sufficient in itself to answer completely the question of whether the Sermon can be fulfilled. Further reflections are necessary. And the question of whether Matthew does not, after all, embody a form of righteousness of works must wait until we interpret his concept of judgement. On this point, within the Sermon on the Mount, the conclusion in 7:13–27 still awaits discussion.

THE WILL OF GOD: ANTITHESES AND RULES OF PIETY (5:17–6:18)

The commandments given in the Antitheses are concrete and extreme in their demands. There are no limits set to the divine will: even the mildest terms of abuse against one's 'brother' are prohibited (5:21–22); no unkindness whatsoever toward him will be condoned. The prohibition of resistance to evil (5:39a) excludes no areas from its sphere of validity; the three explanatory examples cover interpersonal relations (5:39b), legal responsibilities (5:40) and obligations to the occupying forces (5:41). Moreover these examples, which probably originated with Jesus himself, are worded so radically that they seem to permit no forms of 'peaceful' violence: no rebuke for the person who strikes the blow, no legal defence against a plaintiff, no guile against an enemy soldier. The commands are concrete. There is no leeway for interpretation in the prohibition of oaths (5:34, 37). The examples of non-violence given in 5:39b–41, and of loving one's enemy in 5:44b and 5:46–47, are so concrete that neither non-violence nor love of one's enemy can be diluted into a generalized attitude. It need hardly be mentioned that these prohibitions were meant to be followed literally, otherwise Matthew would not have added the proviso 'except in case of unchastity' to the prohibition against divorce in 5:32, a proviso that apparently reflected the customs of his community.

For all these reasons the impression has arisen, with some justification, that the commandments are very exacting, even excessive. This impression is reinforced by the conclusion of the series of Antitheses in verse 48: 'Be perfect, as your Father in Heaven is perfect.' Protestant exegetes, perhaps somewhat too hastily, consigned the perfection Matthew speaks of to mankind's inner nature with a reference to holistic and undivided obedience.[12] As verses 19:21 and 5:20 imply, the point at issue is also, at least in part, complete obedience to the will of God and to all his commandments. The righteousness of the Matthean community must be 'superior' to that of the Pharisees and scribes; the Greek wording makes clear that at least an element of quantity is involved. Precisely verse 5:20 comes noticeably close to what Protestants sense to be 'righteousness of works'. Is the point that the members of the community have a certain 'quota' of righteousness to fulfil, on the basis of which the Son of Man and Judge of the world will grant them entry into the kingdom of heaven?

Several observations can be made to counteract this picture of the ethical substance of the Sermon on the Mount.

First of all it should be mentioned that, for Matthew, *love* is the foremost commandment, and hence the *guiding precept* by which Jesus' other commandments are to be interpreted. Love, for Matthew, is the commandment on which the whole of the Torah hinges (22:40). In the Antitheses he made his view explicit by his choice of placement. The series ends with the commandment to love one's enemy, the sixth Antithesis (5:43–44). But it also begins in the first Antithesis with that same commandment. By adding the injunction to reconcile oneself with one's enemy before coming to trial (5:25f) Matthew made it clear that the 'brother' of the first Antithesis – the man who must not suffer even the mildest abuse – is intended in the same sense. Moreover, the sixth Antithesis interprets the commandment to love one's enemy so as to far transcend personal animosity. The persecutors for whom the disciples are to pray (5:44b) are, of course, the enemies of the community, and thus in Matthew's case the Jews. It was under

[12] See, for example, E. Schweizer, *Das Evangelium nach Matthäus*, *NTD*, 2 (Göttingen: Vandenhoeck & Ruprecht, 1973), 83, who speaks of 'the entire alignment on God, ... not the faultlessness of perfection'.

their hostility that the missionaries of Jesus were made to suffer (see 5:10–12; 10:16–23; 23:34).[13]

How does the commandment to love one's enemy relate to the remaining commandments? How does it relate to the remaining Antitheses, or to the 'jots and tittles' of the Torah (5:18), which will remain valid even until the end of time? Matthew did not reflect systematically upon these questions. He was presumably of the opinion that the love commandment was supreme, that if a conflict should arise among the commandments all the rest should be subordinated to that of love. He seems to have regarded the love commandment as the crown of the commandments, placing demands on mankind beyond what is required by, say, the Decalogue.[14] He probably felt that the laws of ritual, purity, tithing, sacrifice and the sabbath also remained operative, but should be made subordinate to the more significant commandment of love (see 5:18–19, 23–24; 12:7, 11–14; 15:15–20; 23:23–26).

In other words, Matthew does not view the 'righteousness' demanded by God simply in a quantitative sense, as a virtually infinite sum total of rules and strictures. On the contrary, his righteousness has a midpoint. When viewed from this midpoint, God's will is seen to be intelligible. The midpoint also grants men and women obedient to Jesus a certain leeway within which to form their own interpretations and to act in keeping with a given situation. Seen in this light, Jesus' commandments in the Gospel of Matthew are not simply heteronomous norms.

It must be admitted, however, that Matthew only began to foresee the conflicts that might arise between the 'most significant' commandment of the Torah – the commandment of love – and the others. Our experiences with history have shown

[13] Precisely this interpretation of the commandment to love one's enemy clearly shows that it also posed an excessive demand on the Matthean community – even if Matthew may not have been aware of it! See pp. 121–25 below.

[14] Verses 19:16–22, the story of the summoning of the wealthy young man, are directed toward this end. All that this young man lacks of perfection is the radical fulfilment of the love commandment, interpolated by Matthew into the ethical tablets of the Decalogue, with the intention of forcing the rich to give their possessions to the poor. In this respect the love commandment goes one step beyond the Ten Commandments.

that the love commandment can not only stand in conflict with 'religious' commandments – such as those of sacrifice, purity, tithing and the sabbath – but with ethical commandments as well. Not only may it conflict with Old Testament strictures on oaths, divorce or blood-vengeance, it can also fail to coincide with those commandments that are unique to Jesus: the rejection of oaths, the absolute ban on divorce, perhaps even the absolute and consistent renunciation of violence.[15]

The second important clue in this respect is the *exemplarity* of the Matthean commandments. Jesus' commandments very often took the form of generalized propositions, which then had to be made concrete by his listeners themselves, or of examples, for which his listeners were called upon to find analogies in their own lives.[16] Matthew heightens this aspect still further by frequently linking general propositions with concrete examples, thereby stressing the examples' claim to general validity. Thus, in his Gospel, the three proverbs of non-violence (5:39b–41) are explicitly made to serve as examples of a generalized form of behaviour – non-resistance to evil (5:39a). Similarly, the three instructions on alms giving, prayer and fasting (6:2–18) become examples of righteousness practised in secret (6:1). The Antitheses as a whole serve as examples of love, and the commandments in the central section of the Sermon on the Mount become, altogether, examples of active behaviour motivated by love in consonance with the Golden Rule (7:12).

This technique of 'ethics by example' means that the individual commandments in the Sermon on the Mount have a fundamental validity. They far transcend themselves, governing all walks of existence and serving as a guide for life in its entirety. As for the Golden Rule, one might say that it imparts an elemental and universal character to all the commandments

---

[15] This was, in any event, the view held by the Reformation Protestants. They argued that violence as exercised by state and society – the violence, in short, that results from 'secular offices' – was necessary but must be regulated by the principle of love.

[16] A classic instance is found in the three parallel examples of non-violence given in Matthew 5:39b–41. This was, of course, not meant to suggest that the rule only applies to the situations specifically mentioned (e.g. to slaps but not to kicks!). Rather, the commandments are given as examples with a sphere of validity extending far beyond themselves.

given in the Sermon on the Mount. Conversely, the commandments in the Sermon – especially its core, the commandment to
love one's enemy – offer a guide as to how the Golden Rule
should be construed.[17] Taken together, both ensure the ethical
freedom of Jesus' disciples *vis-à-vis* God's will: what 'love your
enemy' means, what 'do as you would have others do to you'
means, cannot be set down normatively but only in the concrete experiences of one's own life. It is precisely this concrete-
ness that, in turn, makes the commandments in the Sermon
humane, transforming their upholders into truly free men and
women rather than imposing excessive demands upon them.

A third point of importance to Matthew's understanding of
the Sermon on the Mount also deserves mention: the idea of
the *path of righteousness* (see 21:32). We first encounter this idea
in 5:20 in the phrase 'superior righteousness', a phrase which,
at first glance, strongly suggests an attitude of 'works'. Reveal-
ingly, the comparative *'perisseus . . . pleionō'* in the clause 'if your
righteousness is not superior' is precisely *not* a superlative.
Instead, it means that Jesus' disciples should do as much as
they can on their path to perfection. The author of the *Didachē*,
a Christian from an early second-century community that was
familiar with Matthew and used him as 'their' gospel, put this
as follows: 'If you can take the entire yoke of the Lord upon
yourself, you will be perfect; if you cannot, do as much as you
are able' (6:2). The phrase that follows concretizes this rule in
reference to dietary strictures: 'Take upon yourself what you
can do.' However, there are certain minima which must be
upheld under all circumstances: 'Beware of the flesh of sacri-
fices to idols!' (6:3). Nor are the Christian fasts on Wednesdays
and Fridays a matter to be freely decided upon by the faithful.

For the Matthean community, too, there is only a *path* to
perfection. Not everyone will attain perfection in the sense
required by the commandments in the Sermon on the Mount.

---

[17] The Golden Rule stands in need of such a guide, without which it can be perverted
to mean the opposite of what Matthew intends. Given a purely formal interpretation, the Golden Rule would not, for example, obligate me to prevent a drunken
driver from climbing into his automobile and driving away, since I would not want
the same to happen to me if I were drunk! The Golden Rule, then, requires a
'canon' for its application.

Not everyone will become a follower of Jesus in the sense that
they will sell their possessions and, like Jesus, itinerantly preach
the kingdom of God. Verses 10:40–42, for example, make clear
that the community consists not only of the wandering
prophets, the righteous and the 'little ones' who form the
subject of the Mission Discourse in chapter 10. There are also
those who remain at home, practising hospitality, clothing the
itinerant missionaries and visiting them in prison (25:31–46),
or giving them a glass of cold water to drink (10:42), thereby
quite surprisingly and unpredictably receiving God's infinite
reward.

The same process can be seen at work in the way Matthew
treats Jesus' classical promise to the itinerant radicals. If men,
they are to be as the birds and not sow and reap; if women, they
are to be as the lilies and not spin and weave. The heavenly
Father, in his infinite love, will provide for them (6:25–33).
Matthew places this promise under the aspect of a general 'rule
of possession' equally applicable to more sedentary Christians:
do not store earthly treasures for you cannot serve both God
and Mammon (6:19–24).

Living in accordance with the Sermon on the Mount is
therefore a *path* to perfection. One should travel this path as far
as possible. On the Day of Judgement the Son of Man will show
just where the minimum righteousness lies that is necessary for
entrance into the kingdom of heaven. In order to travel this
path, the Matthean Jesus makes use primarily of exhortation
rather than laws. The Sermon on the Mount contains
examples, pictorial hyperboles (e.g. 7:2–4) and metaphorical
imperatives (e.g. 5:29–30) to goad its readers into motion. But
it does not set down 'laws'.

Finally, I would like to point out one last dimension to the
Matthean Antitheses which was of great importance to the
evangelist, given the breach between his community and the
synagogues. In 5:17–9 he provided the Antitheses with a 'preamble'. Jesus' Antitheses, as Matthew insists in the presumably
redactional verse 17, do not imply that he has come to abolish
the Law and the prophets. True, his introductory formula –
'You have learned that our forefathers [probably meaning the

Sinai generation] were told [probably meaning by the Bible] ... but what I tell you is this' – invites such a conclusion by counterposing his own words to those of the Torah. For Matthew, however, this is not the case. Jesus' Antitheses mean for him a *heightening of the Torah* and by no means its abolition.

Matthew does not say how in particular he connects this thought with the Antitheses. Basically, we must recall that the Torah was a living entity for Judaism at that time. Neither Hillel, who abolished a rule regarding the sabbath year as being dangerous and impractical, nor the author of the Temple Scroll, who wrote a new version of the Mosaic Law on Mount Sinai, nor the Essenes in Qumran, who, like Jesus, rejected private oaths and presumably also divorce, felt that their decisions 'abolished' the Torah. On the contrary, part of the enduring existence of the Torah in Judaism at that time was its living quality and its amenability to change. Seen in this light, Jesus' ethics were reconcilable with a *living* Torah, and Matthew did not suffer from a lack of precedent for what Jesus demanded as the will of God.

Jesus' uniqueness more likely resided in the fact that, astonishingly, he did *not* derive his ethic of the kingdom of God from the Torah, no matter how compatible the two may have been. Nor did he appeal to the authority of Moses. In this way he set in train a development among his disciples which led to the supposition that he fundamentally, if not in practice, abolished the Torah. It was probably this development – or, more precisely, Hellenistic Christianity and its turn toward the Gentiles – that provoked the Jews to accuse Jesus of undermining the Law and the prophets.

Matthew is fully aware that Jesus is the ultimate and immediate arbiter for interpreting the will of God. He speaks with authority, not like the scribes (7:29). He is the 'sole teacher' (23:8). On the other hand, Matthew is inspired by a basic conviction that Jesus, far from revoking the Torah and the prophets, himself represents its zenith and culmination (5:17). He 'fulfils' them, satisfying their commandments in every respect and teaching them accordingly. This basic conviction is fundamental to Matthew because it is fully consistent with his belief that Jesus' disciples – that is, Matthew himself and his community – represent the true Israel. For this reason he *had* to raise a fundamental claim to the legacy of Israel, including its Law, and to insist with polemical urgency to the Israelite majority, led by the Pharisees and dismissive of Jesus, that it was Jesus who fulfilled the Torah and the prophets. On the other hand, he could not subordinate Jesus to the Torah like a scribe, as though he were a mere interpreter. It was these two convictions that led him to formulate his principle sharply, 'Do not think that I have come to abolish the law and the prophets; I did not come to abolish, but to fulfil' (5:17). This sentence contains both thoughts: Jesus' obligations to the heritage of Israel, and his fundamental sovereignty, which allows him to determine what the meaning of that heritage is. To Matthew, the sentence forms a guideline to the interpretation of the Antitheses. It reveals the only way, for a Jewish–Christian like himself following the breach with the synagogue, that Jesus' Antitheses can be understood.[18]

THE JUDGEMENT (7:13–27)

The Sermon on the Mount ends with a forward glance to the Last Judgement. In this respect it resembles other Matthean discourses (see 13:36–43, 47–49; 18:23–35; 24:29 – 25:46). As in those discourses it is the dark colours of this prospect that predominate. Few will discover the 'road of sorrows'[19] that leads through the narrow gate to life (7:13–14). The solemn words spoken by the Judge of the world in 7:23 are words of condemnation. The double metaphor of the house builders ends in 7:27 with an image of rain, tempest and calamity. In

---

[18] In other words, I do not feel that the basic principle expressed in Matthew 5:17 is directed primarily against the Christian Antinomians, as does G. Barth, 'Matthew's Understanding of the Law', in G. Bornkamm et al, *Tradition* (cf. n. 21, ch. 1), 159–64. This would mean that 5:17–20 has two recipients, with Matthew first taking issue with Christian Antinomians and then, in verse 20, with the Jewish leaders. However, 5:17–20 is not a complex of two polemical asides but rather, in view of the rift between synagogues and communities, a theological declaration of a fundamental principle.

[19] *Tethlimmenē* means 'full of *thlipseis*'.

7:19 Matthew has Jesus proclaim a saying of John the Baptist: every tree that fails to bear good fruit will be cut down and cast into the fire. Indeed, the parallels that Matthew sees between Jesus' and the Baptist's sermons of judgement and atonement are striking.[20] He seems to think nothing of the popular Christian notion that John gave priority to judgement and Jesus to salvation.

The judgement under discussion here is a judgement of works. The question of whether to cut down the tree is decided on the basis of its fruit (7:20). Matthew makes no distinction between the deeds of Christians who fail the ordeal of judgement, and those same Christians as individuals, who may escape 'as if through fire' (as Paul put it in 1 Cor. 3:15). On the contrary, it is their deeds alone that determine their fate as individuals. This becomes clear in the example of the false prophets, with whom the evangelist takes issue in a concluding sentence: 'Not everyone who calls me "Lord, Lord" will enter the kingdom of heaven, but only those who do the will of my heavenly Father' (7:21). Our personal relation to the heavenly Lord Jesus, the inspiration he gives us for prophecy, the charisma he grants us for mighty deeds and exorcisms – none of this will be decisive on the Day of Judgement, only our works. What is more, this applies equally to Christians and non-Christians alike; it is striking that the epilogue of the Sermon on the Mount makes no distinction between members of the Church and the rest of humankind. To put it bluntly, it is not faith that determines whether we are saved or damned, but works. This curt conclusion leads us back to the question of whether the entire Sermon on the Mount might not be an attempt to motivate men and women to prepare their own salvation by proceeding consistently along the path of righteousness.

The regularity with which Jesus' discourses in Matthew end with a warning about the Last Judgement also prevents us from adopting a convenient theological escape. Obviously their point is not simply to make the members of the Christian

[20] Also compare 3:2 with 4:17.

community toe the line by threatening judgement upon them for their waning zeal and their susceptibility to false prophets, sometimes called 'Antinomians'.[21] Nor is the point to rekindle their feelings with threats now that their Christian charity has 'grown cold' (24:12). For Matthew, the idea of judgement is more than an exhortatory line of argument which must leap into action whenever other linguistic devices of preaching fail.

However, this does not make the basic problems of Matthew's annunciations of the Last Judgement any simpler – on the contrary. It is far from my intention to resolve them already here and precipitously reclaim Matthew for a theology of grace. In an earlier section[22] I tried to present and retrace the lines of grace in Matthew's thought. Do they ultimately subsume the Matthean theology of judgement? Only a backward glance at the whole of Matthew's theology of judgement can answer this question.[23] At this point I would only like to venture a few brief observations within the framework of the Sermon on the Mount. There are three of them:

(1) 'Pass no judgement lest you be judged', writes Matthew in 7:1. These words of admonition presuppose that there will be a Judgement. They do not see the Judgement as an eventuality which may possibly come about if the disciples allow themselves to be misled into passing judgement (see 7:2). It is, therefore, precisely the idea of judgement that prevents men and women from passing judgement and enables them to love.

(2) Matthew deals freely with the notion of a 'reward' promised in heaven to those who gain entrance (5:12, 46; 6:1–16; 20:1–16). But nowhere does he suggest that this 'reward' is something which human beings can earn. On the contrary, the Beatitudes clearly construe the 'reward' as something held in pledge. Verse 10:42 virtually over-emphasizes the disproportion of this reward: the reward for a single glass of cold water is – paradise. This is also the underlying thought (Jesus' thought!) behind the parable of the workers in the vineyard in 20:1–16. Lastly, looking ahead in my discussion, I should mention the element of surprise that undergirds the

[21] See n. 18 above.   [22] See pp. 46–51 and 152 above.
[23] See pp. 129–32 below.

great Matthean scene of the judgement of the sheep and the goats (25:31–46). Those who visited, fed and clothed the 'least of my brothers' are amazed to discover the immense repercussions of their human deeds.

(3) It is basic to Matthew's idea of judgement that the community is apparently not given precedence a priori on Judgement Day. All human beings, whether members of the community or not, are faced with the temptation of the 'wide road' (7:13–14). No precedence is given to community members over the 'wolves in sheep's clothing' (7:15) who molest them. True, the false prophets will not be able to rely on their charismatic powers. But neither will the Christians addressed by Matthew be able to counteract them with reference to their spiritual possessions, not even a confession of faith in their 'Lord'. All that ultimately matters are their works. Before the Judge, all lances are of equal length. The sole advantage granted to readers of Matthew's Gospel is that the evangelist tells them precisely that. In other words, Matthew rehearses with his readers the absolute sovereignty of the Judge of the world, against whom there are no demands that can possibly be raised, but only *his* assessment of human deeds.

Everything will culminate in the question of who this Judge of the world is, that he be accorded such absolute power. To Matthew this question is already answered. It is Jesus: the same who is now God's Immanuel and the travelling companion of the community, the same who is now proclaiming God's commandments to the community, and who is leading them in prayer to their Father in heaven.

CHAPTER 4

The ministry of the Messiah and his disciples in Israel (Matthew 8:1 – 11:30)

MATTHEW'S GOSPEL AS AN INCLUSIVE STORY OF JESUS

In 8:1, after Jesus has proclaimed his programme on the Mount, the Matthean story of Jesus sets out in earnest. Matthew now begins to relate how Jesus healed the sick among God's people (see 4:23). This forms the subject of chapters 8 and 9. Jesus returns to this subject at the opening of chapter 11 (11:5–6). In between, in chapter 10, is the so-called Discourse on Mission, in which Jesus sends his disciples forth to Israel with the same authority and commission as his own. They are told to proclaim the kingdom of God, as he had done in chapters 5 to 7,[1] and to heal the sick, as he had done in chapters 8 and 9. At first glance, therefore, it would seem that chapters 5 to 11 form a unit. But the end of chapter 11 goes beyond the previous subject matter. Jesus delivers a quite harsh address to the people, who have fully accepted neither him nor John the Baptist. The people become 'this generation', resembling children who cannot decide whether they want to play wedding or funeral and therefore do neither (11:16–19). This address is followed by Jesus' denunciation of Capernaum, Bethsaida and Chorazin, which is all the more surprising as these towns have done him no harm till now. On the contrary, in Capernaum, Jesus' 'own town' (9:1), he was greeted by throngs of people (8:1, 18; 9:8). These throngs were not hostile to Jesus; indeed, their reaction is summarized in 9:33 as 'Nothing like this has ever been seen in Israel!' It is thus all the more striking that

[1] Compare 4:17 and 10:7.

62

Jesus, in 11:20–24, grimly threatens these Galilean towns with destruction. This menacing pericope is offset by a pericope of promise in 11:25–30. Here Jesus thanks his Father for revealing himself to the simple and pledges that he, the Son of God, shall reveal his Father to the elect (11:25–27). This passage points to the final lines of the Gospel, Jesus' revelation on the Galilean mountaintop,[2] which is likewise preceded by a 'negative' passage on the Jews (28:11–15, 16–20). There is good reason to regard 11:25–27 as the conclusion of a main section of the Gospel.

Chapter 11, then, intrudes unexpectedly and abruptly within the thread of Matthew's story. Similar oddities can be noticed on the narrative surface in chapters 8 and 9. In 8:10 Jesus says, 'Nowhere in Israel have I found such faith', although his ministry in Israel had just begun and till now there had been no mention whatsoever either of faith or lack of faith. His subsequent withdrawal with his disciples to the opposite shore seems unmotivated: after all, not only did he 'sight' the crowds (8:18), he had already healed the sick among them. Suddenly, in 10:1, there are twelve disciples although up to that point only five had been mentioned. Equally strange is the way events follow upon one another in quick succession: chapters 8 and 9 convey the impression that Jesus healed the sick without interruption. Each story emerges directly from its predecessor; Matthew offers a narrative thread without a single break in time or place. At its conclusion is the dual response of the people and the Pharisees to Jesus' healings, summarizing chapters 8 and 9 (9:33–34). Although the people's response is positive, the Pharisees accuse Jesus of driving out demons in the name of the devil. This, too, comes as a surprise: not only have the Pharisees had nothing negative to say until now about Jesus' miraculous healings – their only appearance has been in connection with the dispute over sharing a table with tax-gatherers and sinners (9:9–13) – but Jesus has, up to this point, only cast out a single demon (9:32–33).

---

2 There are several catchwords in common: *panta (par)edothē, ouranos – gē.*

There are two things to conclude from our observations. First, Matthew is obviously interested in fashioning a coherent narrative. The stories of chapters 8 and 9 are not simply a sample anthology of miracles arranged by topic, as was once believed, particularly under the influence of the important study by H. J. Held.[3] Rather, Matthew wishes to depict a historical progression culminating in the dual response of the people and Pharisees to Jesus' miracles.

On the other hand, Matthew is seemingly unconcerned about coherence on the narrative surface. Again and again strange and unexpected things happen. Again and again Jesus and his adversaries are surprisingly harsh in their response.

This observation can be further pursued with a line of thought we obtain when we view the Gospel diachronically. In chapters 8 and 9 Matthew fashions his narrative thread by interweaving two quite different sections from the Gospel of Mark: 1:40 – 2:22 and 4:35 – 5:43. Into this construction he then interpolates two miracle stories from the Sayings Source (Q 7:1–10; 11:14–15) and another from a later chapter of Mark (10:46–52 = Matt. 9:27–31). The final two miracle stories are duplicated: Matthew later repeats them in varied form as new stories. Earlier, in the Gospel of Mark, the miracle stories had been arranged in chronological order. Matthew destroys this sequence in order to create a new one of his own. Did he feel that his order was more correct, that the events took place in the sequence given in his own Gospel and not in the order he received from Mark? Most likely this question did not interest him in the slightest as he created his own sequence.

What did interest him? What does this chronological sequence mean? I would like to propose the following *thesis*: Matthew arranged his story of Jesus according to an 'internal principle'. He told it as the story of Jesus' conflict with Israel. Jesus began his ministry in Israel, among the people; he healed the sick among God's people; he summoned his first disciples

---

[3] See H. J. Held, 'Matthew as Interpreter of the Miracle Stories', in G. Bornmann et al, *Tradition* (cf. n. 21, ch. 1), esp. 165–210. Verses 8:1–17 are primarily concerned with Jesus as 'saviour', verses 8:18 to 9:17 with discipleship. Faith is the subject of 9:18–31 (see *ibid.*, 248–49).

from the people. At the same time, the first tensions begin to arise between him and the leaders of the people, above all the Pharisees. These form the contents of chapters 8 and 9. This thesis finds support in the Mission Discourse in chapter 10, where Jesus sends forth his disciples solely and exclusively to Israel (10:5–6). Chapter 11 represents a backward glance and summing up that already anticipates the future. The tensions will increase: Jesus will encounter rejection in Israel; a group of disciples will form in Israel to whom the Son will reveal the secret of the Father. This is one anticipation of the end of the Gospel. Another is the reference to the faith of the Gentile centurion in Capernaum, of which there was no equivalent in Israel. In passages such as these Matthew intimates the goal of his story.

Matthew will continue to narrate his story of Jesus as the story of the conflict with Israel. The next large section, from 12:1 to 16:20, deals mainly with the repeated withdrawals of Jesus and his disciples, made necessary by the hostility of Israel's leaders. Verses 16:21 to 20:34 then take up the life of the new community that has now arisen in Israel as a result of these withdrawals – the Church. Verses 21:1 to 25:46 will unfold Jesus' great and final reckoning, in the holy city of Jerusalem, with Israel's disobedient leaders and the people they have misled. These same verses will conclude with a final address by Jesus to the community from which they are to draw learning. The story of the passion, in chapters 26 to 28, then shows how the Jewish leaders apparently assert themselves against Jesus, the coming Judge of the world, whereas in reality his death and resurrection merely make plain Israel's fateful embroilment in guilt and lies. The Gospel again ends with two mutually antithetical pericopes. On one side are the 'Jews' (28:15), who 'to this day' cannot comprehend the truth of Jesus' resurrection. On the other is the resurrected Lord, who, from the mountaintop in Galilee, sends his disciples forth to the Gentiles (28:19–20).

This, in abbreviated form, is the 'inner thread' of Matthew's story of Jesus in its main stages. Why did Matthew write this story? Why did he partly rearrange and expand the narrative outline of the Gospel of Mark in order to work out this conflict? Recalling what we said earlier about the history of the Matthean community,[4] we realize that this story of Jesus mirrors the community's own story. It, too, was once part of Israel. It, too, proclaimed the kingdom of God in Israel and healed the sick in the name of Jesus (5:11–12; 10:23; 23:34). It, too, then withdrew from the land of Israel to the northern land of Syria, a heathen country. It, too, had to find new bearings following the breach with the synagogues and to reach a reckoning with Israel. And now, in the narrative present, the risen Lord is sending them to the Gentiles. The experiences of the disciples with Jesus mirror their own experiences with the resurrected Lord. The story of Jesus mirrors their own story,[5] making their story transparent. It is in this sense that I wish to call the entire Gospel of Matthew an 'inclusive story'.

THE MIRACLE STORIES

But it is not only Matthew's story of Jesus as a whole that is transparent of the present. The same applies to the separate strands in the Gospel's source traditions, and especially to the miracle stories. Redaction critics of the Bible have rediscovered what Church exegetes had known all along: the miracle stories tell not only of events that happened 'back then' in the past history of Jesus, but also of 'our own' experiences.

The best-known example[6] is the story of the calming of the storm, which Matthew connects with two paradigms of discipleship from the Sayings Source (Q 8:18–27). Jesus wishes to go to the opposite shore of the lake. He is approached by two men who want to follow him. The first of them, a scribe, is told by Jesus that the Son of Man has nowhere to lay his head. The other, who is already a disciple, wishes to bury his father first. Jesus then boards the boat, followed by his disciples. The

---

[4] See pp. 17–21 above.

[5] There is a certain similarity here with John 1–12, though it cannot be sustained in detail, as was attempted by R. Brown in *The Community of the Beloved Disciple* (New York: Paulist, 1979).

[6] See G. Bornkamm, 'The Stilling of the Storm in Matthew', in G. Bornkamm et al, *Tradition* (cf. n. 21, ch. 1), 52–57.

calming of the ensuing storm mirrors the later experiences of discipleship. The little boat recalls the ship of life.[7] Storms symbolize danger or death. One cannot say for certain what Matthew's readers may have thought as they read of the earthquake and the waves breaking over the prow: the text gives free reign to the imagination. The disciples address Jesus, seated in the boat, in the language of fervent prayer: 'Save us, Lord!' At the words 'we are sinking' the Greek text alludes to Apocalyptic perdition. In short, Matthew's readers project this miracle story onto their own experiences. They may have thought of their own lives, of illness, death or material want, or of the experiences of their community, perhaps the persecutions they suffered. They probably recalled how the Lord had helped them in a time of need. The miracle story expands with the adding of their own experiences, becoming expressive of them. It sets the directions in which this expansion may occur, but it is not self-contained. It is more important that the story provide opportunities for associations from one's own life than that it prevent such associations. The context links these experiences to the community: what happens here, in the boat, is about to be undergone by the community of Jesus' followers as their own boat departs from the shore on which many people are standing. Thus the miracle story is, in turn, 'inclusive'. Its concern is not only the historical Jesus, but at the same time the present 'Lord', who will accompany the community to the end of time.

In this sense I would like to argue on behalf of a 'symbolic' explication of Matthew's miracle stories. Almost all of them are designed to mean more than they say: they transcend past events in the story of Jesus and enter one's own life, encouraging personal experiences with Jesus or making such experiences intelligible. This is entirely evident in the case of the second calming of the storm, related in Matthew 14:22–33. Here he has inserted into the Marcan story the episode of Peter

[7] Besides this widespread metaphor, ancient literary texts also contain the metaphor of the ship of state, which, however, Matthew is unlikely to have drawn upon. The Christian metaphor of the 'ship of the community' has no predecessors in the source tradition and presumably originated in this passage.

walking on the water toward his Lord (14:28–31). Faced with
the overwhelming force of the waves, Peter takes fright and
again cries out, 'Save me, Lord!'. Jesus holds his protective
hand over him and says: 'How little faith you have. Why did
you hesitate?' Both stories of the calming of the storm contain
the words 'little faith'. Matthew found it in the Sayings Source
(*Q* 12:28) and employed it several times in his Gospel. 'Little
faith' is the faith of those who set out with Jesus only to lose
heart. Little faith is faith mingled with fear and doubt. Little
faith is the faith of those who would like to believe but cannot.
Matthew apparently felt this situation to be typical of his
community.

Equally transparent to the community, though in a different
way, are the stories of the healing of the blind. These stories are
especially frequent in Matthew. In Jewish tradition 'blind'
refers not only to physical blindness but to spiritual blindness
as well: to be blind means to be unenlightened, or to live in the
darkness of the old aeon. The sense of being led by Jesus from
blindness to knowledge is an experience shared by the readers
of Matthew's Gospel. Already Mark's story of the blind Bartimaeus, who is healed in order to follow Jesus on his path to
Jerusalem (Mark 10:46–52), must be interpreted metaphorically. Matthew plays on the word 'blind' by allowing Jesus to
heal the blind again and again (9:27–31; 12:22–24; 20:29–34;
21:14) and, conversely, to refer to the Pharisees as blind leaders
(15:14; 23:16–26). These stories, too, grow to accommodate the
experiences of Matthew's own community.

It need hardly be said that the same applies to those stories
that speak of 'faith' (8:5–13; 9:20–22, 27–31; cf. 17:20–21). In
Matthew, the story of the healing of the lame man in 9:2–8
becomes directly transparent for, or expressive of, the forgiveness of sins experienced by the community. Jesus, the Son
of Man, endowed with the authority to forgive sins (9:6),
continues to exercise this authority in his community. This
explains why, at the end of the story, the crowd (symbolic of
the community) praises God 'for granting such authority to
men' (9:8) and for allowing them to experience it in, for
example, the Holy Communion (26:28). The two stories of the

feeding of the multitudes, told by Matthew in 14:13–21 and 15:32–39, contain a wide range of potential meanings on which readers can project their own experiences. They can recall their own experiences of want and satiety, and perhaps their dreams of plenitude and superfluity. Most of all, however, they can recall what they themselves experience with Jesus at the Eucharist. The recollection of the introductory words of the Last Supper, words familiar to them all, spring to mind. Once again, these texts are not primarily intended to circumvent free associations – to preclude personal experiences and 'wrong' interpretation – but rather to evoke such associations in order to give rise to a welter of potential meanings. Indeed, perhaps the only interpretation of such a text that might be considered 'wrong' is one that excludes personal experiences with Jesus.

Yet Matthew's miracle stories are, of course, also relevant to the present in a direct sense. The Matthean community, too, witnessed miracles, as is made plain in 17:19–20. For Matthew, 'little faith' also means doubting one's own authority to work miracles. In the Sending of the Twelve in 10:7–8, Jesus' commission to the disciples to heal the sick and cast out demons is given more space than his instruction to proclaim God's message. The history of the exegesis of these verses has suppressed this fact to an astonishing degree.[8] That Jesus first healed Israel's sick and cast out its demons is significant to Matthew not only because it thereby demonstrates that Israel truly experienced all that the Messiah is capable of accomplishing. No, the real importance lay elsewhere. For the miracles embodied a true core of the mission of Jesus and his community: 'salvation' – healing – takes place, if not exclusively, then at least initially in the realm of the corporeal. The community experienced the presence of the exalted Lord in its midst equally in the fact that here, too, the sick became well and the possessed were made free.

Till now we have spoken of the 'symbolic' explication of Matthew's miracle stories. It is now time to make this term more precise. To view miracle stories symbolically does not

---

[8] See U. Luz, *Das Evangelium nach Matthäus II*, *EKK*, I/2 (Neukirchen-Vluyn: Neukirchener, 1990), 94.

mean, according to Matthew, to transport them from the realm of the corporeal to a realm of the spirit. Rather, it means that the corporeal realm recounted in the miracles goes above and beyond itself. The corporeal miracle is, as it were, the hub of meaning for an event that affects men and women as a whole, including their spirit. To view miracle stories symbolic-ally, then, does not mean that they did not really happen and must therefore be transported to a symbolic level lest they become meaningless. Just as the spiritual interpretation of the Scripture by the later Church never superseded its literal interpretation, the present-day significance of a miracle story never superseded, for Matthew, the fact that it really did once occur, namely, during Jesus' lifetime.

It need hardly be stressed that Matthew did not distinguish between past and present with the detachment of a modern historian. For him there was no question that Jesus really did work the miracles reported of him. Matthew and his commu-nity, after all, experienced in their own lives that those things recorded in the miracle stories continue to exercise their influ-ence in manifold ways. The merging of the past report and present experience of Jesus corresponds to the merging of the earthly Immanuel and the Lord as present in his community (1:23; 28:20). The experiences undergone by Matthew and his community, initiated by Jesus' miracles, were signs that the Lord really is with his community 'always to the end of time'. Thus, the transparence of Matthew's miracle stories – their open-endedness and direct relevance to future readers – is fully in keeping with his Christology.

THE SON OF DAVID AS A WORKER OF MIRACLES

The title 'Son of David' occurs frequently in the miracle stories. In chapters 8 and 9 it is the two blind men who address Jesus as the Son of David and plead for his mercy (9:27). The same pattern is repeated in 20:30–31. Here Matthew was inspired by Mark's story of blind Bartimaeus, where the same title is used (Mark 10:47–48). Jesus is similarly addressed as Son of David by the Phoenician woman – a Gentile – who awaits salvation for her daughter from the Messiah of Israel. Just how significant this is for Matthew is shown in 12:23, where the crowd reacts to Jesus' acts of exorcism by asking whether he is the Son of David, while the Pharisees accuse him of complicity with the devil.

There is little to be gained from inquiring into the roots of the 'Son of David' title in religious history.[9] Matthew makes plain his own understanding of this expression through his story. In the Prologue the title quite clearly had a 'genealogical' significance: Jesus, through his adoption by Joseph, truly is the Son of David and for this very reason a claimant for the title of Israel's King–Messiah (1:18 – 2:12). Matthew therefore engages his Jewish–Christian readers at the level of their own expectations of the Messiah.[10] None the less, he now tells them a story that does not quite fit their customary images of the Son of David. It is not a story of wars and acts of political liberation, but one of healings and love. Matthew's Son of David therefore behaves differently from the way Jewish readers expected him to behave, despite the fact that, genealogically, he truly is the Son of David. The story of Jesus thwarts Jewish expectations of the Son of David. If the title 'Son of David' is heard time and again in connection with miracles, if he is addressed as 'Son of David' by a Gentile woman and by the uneducated, but not by the Pharisees, the readers of Matthew's Gospel are given to understand that this is a Son of David of a quite particular kind. He is a liberator of simple people, a liberator from disease and material want. It is precisely the scribes and the leaders of the people who do not acknowledge him as the Son of David, and precisely the suffering and the uneducated who do (21:9, 15).[11] In this sense, and no other,

---

9 K. Berger, in 'Die königlichen Messiastraditionen des Neuen Testaments', *NT.S* 20 (1973–74), 3–9, thinks of another son of David, Solomon, who likewise held sway over the demons with his powers of exorcism, according to the late Testament of Solomon.

10 The first documented occurrence of the 'Son of David' title is in Pss.Sol. 17:21. After that it occurs relatively often in early rabbinical texts roughly contemporary with Matthew.

11 Strikingly, it is precisely Jesus' healings that are categorically rejected by the leaders of Israel: see 9:34, 12:24ff., 38ff. and 16:1ff. (after 15:29–39).

Jesus *is* the Son of David and Israel's Messiah. His concern is the corporeal and spiritual salvation of God's people, of Israel. The title 'Son of David' is therefore intended to emphasize that Jesus is the Messiah of Israel, but in such a way that he modifies Israel's expectations. In contrast to Jewish expectations, Jesus' quality as Son of David shifts messianic hopes from the political to the human level. This explains why, for Matthew, the miracles are a demonstration of Jesus' messiahship.

Throughout the Gospel of Matthew the title 'Son of David' is linked to the fate of Israel. For Matthew it is highly significant that the Phoenician woman – a Gentile – uses the title, thereby appealing to Israel's Messiah (15:22). In his response Jesus reverts to his earlier saying in 10:6: he was sent to the 'lost sheep of the house of Israel, and to them alone' (15:24). Yet the woman addresses Jesus as 'Lord' and 'does homage' to him in much the same way as the Gentile Magi had done (2:11) and as the disciples also do to their Lord (14:33; 28:9, 17). It is not merely Jesus' reservations that she overcomes with her faith; Matthew's concern is not simply, as with Mark, that Israel be 'first' to partake of salvation (Mark 7:27a). Rather, his concern is that the fundamental difference separating Israel and the Gentiles be surmounted in this story. This brings us to another possible interpretation of Matthew's miracle stories: they may refer 'symbolically' to the unfolding of the *Heilsgeschichte*, the history of God's actions in the world and of mankind's salvation. In so doing Matthew, like the Old Church at a later date, can even make use of allegory. The 'dogs' and 'children' in 15:26 must be interpreted allegorically.[12] The 'Son of David' title points to this dimension of the story.

The story of the Canaanite woman in 15:21–28 is not the only one which must be understood in this way. It is closely paralleled by 8:5–13, the healing of the centurion's son in

---

[12] When Matthew calls the Gentiles 'little dogs' he is by no means displaying the contempt felt by a pious Jew toward Gentile 'dogs'. It is not the despised stray mongrels but domesticated housedogs that form the subject of the well-known image in Mark 7:27–28 par. However, by referring to 10:5–6 and omitting the Marcan *prōton*, Matthew makes clear that for him there is a *difference in kind* between Israelites and Gentiles, with the former having not just an initial but an exclusive claim to God's salvation.

Capernaum. Here, too, the point is that a single episode foretells the future salvation of the Gentiles as a whole. In this respect it has the character of a 'signal'. Matthew has declared this to be his principle by interpolating a passage on the Judgement from the Sayings Source (Q 13:28–29), Jesus' menacing words against 'those born to the kingdom', who may find themselves excluded from the eschatological table and the company of the patriarchs of Israel. In the context of Matthew's Gospel these words become a proclamation of disaster foretelling what actually will happen, since the vast majority of Israel did not find faith in Jesus. The story of the healing of the two Gadarenes in 8:28–34 has a similar function as a signal. Matthew is, of course, perfectly aware that the mighty town of Gadara, then an important centre of philosophy, is a Gentile city. For this very reason he omits the ending of the Marcan story given in Mark 5:18–20: the two healed men are not yet permitted to preach in the Decapolis, for the time of the Gentile mission is yet to come. Thus, our story is an unambiguous signal for something that will take place later in the history of mankind's salvation.

It is also fitting that the 'Son of David' passages become more frequent the closer we come to Jesus' entrance into the holy city of Jerusalem (20:30–31; 21:9, 15). Now it is crowds – the blind, the 'children' and 'simple people' of Israel – who acclaim Jesus as the Son of David, as their Messiah, and acknowledge him as a prophet.[13] The 'little people' in Israel, then, recognize Jesus for what he is; they receive the miracles bestowed by the healing Messiah upon his people and respond to them. Opposite them stand, menacingly, the high priests and scribes, now in the precincts of their own temple (21:15–16). They will have absolutely nothing to do with the miracles of the Son of David; their only concern is that this man has, with his healings, created a place for himself in the hearts of the people. The reason for their opposition is, accord-

---

[13] In 21:10 Matthew deliberately distinguishes the 'crowds' (verse 8f. and 11, with adversative *de*) from the restrained and unresponsive 'entire city'. The townspeople of Jerusalem are not the 'crowd' that welcome Jesus as the 'Son of David' and 'prophet from Galilee' during his entrance.

ing to Matthew, the popular acclaim that Jesus attained with his healings. This is fully consistent with the image that Jesus' adversaries have made of him till now: from the very outset the Pharisees are convinced that he is in league with the devil (9:34; 12:24). The reason why they accuse Jesus is, as intimated by the juxtaposition of 12:23 and 12:24, precisely that the people see in him the Son of David, and thus begin to question the Pharisees' claims to leadership. Hardly has he arrived than they wish to have him put to death (12:14) for no reason at all, simply as a response to the fact that he is performing good deeds in Israel. The 'high priests and scribes' who reappear in 21:15 are already familiar to Matthew's readers from 2:4 as Herod's henchmen. Nothing good can be expected of them; they are 'evil' by definition. That this is an unjust view of the Pharisees and of Jesus' other Jewish opponents will occupy us later.

Jesus responds to the accusations of his adversaries by quoting the Scripture: 'Have you never read that text, "Thou hast made children and babes at the breast sound aloud thy praise"?' (21:16). That the miracles of the Son of David are accepted by the little people of Israel and rejected by the great is God's will as witnessed in the Scripture. The written witness is clear and unambiguous; the opposition of the great is baseless and malevolent. Thus, the final pericope in Matthew's Gospel to mention the title 'Son of David' likewise shows the Pharisees ensnared in a contradiction with their own Scripture (22:41–46). Jesus confronts them with the question of the Messiah. They answer that the Messiah is the Son of David.[14] Jesus continues his line of questioning with the aid of a passage from David's own Psalms: the Messiah is *kyrios*, 'lord'. What does that mean? How can David call his own son 'lord'? Matthew's community, of course, knows what it means, for they honour Jesus as their 'Lord' and profess their belief that he sits at the right hand of God. They understand the Scripture. The Pharisees however do not, and fall silent. According to Matthew, the only way truly to understand the Scripture is

---

[14] See Gnilka, *Matthäusevangelium II* (cf. n. 20, ch. 1), 254–55: 'Their response is, one might say, an academic one.'

from a Christian viewpoint. For the Pharisees the Scripture must forever remain a riddle.

Thus, the stories of Jesus' miracles, and the 'Son of David' title so closely connected with them, serve in Matthew's Gospel to relate the conflict with Israel and hence the 'plot' of his story. Israel's Messiah, Matthew tells us, is Jesus, the healing Messiah of the little people of that nation. That he is the Son of David is a temporary insight that must be pursued more fully to a profession of belief in the 'Lord', who sits at the right hand of God and disposes over all powers in heaven and on earth. The high priests and Pharisees have maliciously closed their ears to this insight and disparaged Israel's Messiah. Their contradiction with the Bible should, by now at least, have made clear to them the reality of their predicament.

THE MISSION DISCOURSE (MATTHEW 10)

The second discourse in Matthew's Gospel, the Discourse on Mission, is woven especially tightly into the narrative thread of his Jesus story. The two sayings of Jesus that bracket its first section at 10:5–6 and 10:23, limiting the mission of the disciples to Israel, let us know where we are in Matthew's story – at the beginning, when Jesus devoted his love exclusively to God's chosen people. But even in this opening section it becomes clear that Jesus' words apply not only to the past. Verse 10:18, for example, already points to the later ministry to the Gentiles, and 24:9–14 will reveal that the disciples' sufferings in Israel, mentioned in 10:17–23, are to be repeated among the Gentiles. Thus, what Jesus said to his disciples in the past retains a fundamental importance. The ban on travel gear in 10:9–10 is updated by Matthew to become a 'ban on acquisition', primarily intended to prevent Jesus' missionaries from using the preaching of the gospel as a means of making money. For their labours on behalf of the gospel Jesus' emissaries are to receive nothing more than *nourishment*.[15] This shift of emphasis in Matthew was warranted by experiences made at that time

---

[15] *Trophē* (nourishment) in 10:10 is redactional.

with wandering missionaries, Christian and non-Christian alike.[16] The ban on travel gear provides an example of the way in which Matthew imparts contemporary relevance to Jesus' sayings; this presupposes, of course, that they were meant to be heard in the present. Especially in the second part of the Mission Discourse, in verses 24–42, there is not the slightest indication that the Jesus sayings collected there are meant to apply only to the historical Jesus. Thus, the same can be said of the Mission Discourse as of all of Jesus' discourses in Matthew: they are 'spoken to the winds', addressing the reader directly and applying to the community in the present.

From a literary viewpoint this is accomplished very deftly at the end of the discourse. Although Jesus dispatches the twelve apostles, they do not actually leave the scene. In Matthew's Gospel – unlike Mark 6:7–30, and especially unlike Luke 10:1–20 – the dispatching of the Twelve at Jesus' behest does not take place. Once Jesus has sent forth his disciples to preach they remain where they are. Instead, Jesus himself sets out and preaches in the cities of Israel (11:1). The Mission Discourse is thus a manifesto of principles on Jesus' part. It wishes to tell us about preaching and church *per se*.

This line of thought is especially important for our assessment of the itinerant radicals. Matthew has Jesus dispatch his disciples as wandering missionaries, bereft of goods and protection, like sheep among the wolves. Such statements, when understood in relation to the contemporary Church, have been an embarrassment to virtually every subsequent church throughout history. The Matthean Discourse on Mission burdens ecclesiastical officials of later centuries with the question of why they themselves are no longer poor and persecuted, bereft of goods and homeland, why they themselves no longer heal the sick, and so on. Faced with these questions, it was convenient for them to reply that the Mission Discourse dealt,

---

[16] A non-Christian warning against greedy missionaries can be found in Menander (*Sent.* 43). Lucian's diatribe against Peregrinus pillories a comparable case among Christian 'money-grubbers' (*Mort.* 11–16). The *Didachē*, which originated in a Matthean community, urges wariness against greedy itinerant apostles and prophets (11:5–6, 9, 12).

of course, solely with the situation in Jesus' own day, and that circumstances since then have considerably changed.[17] In this way the discourse can easily be neutralized and its questions parried. According to such interpretations, which are still held today,[18] itinerant radicalism was merely a phenomenon of the early days of the Church and not a fundamental question regarding its institutional fabric. In the history of biblical exegesis the Matthean Discourse on Mission was taken up and seriously adopted almost exclusively by radical minorities, among whom the marginal groups and mendicant friars of the late Middle Ages and the Anabaptists of the Age of Reformation deserve special mention.

Notwithstanding all attempts by the Church to blunt these instructions, it is important to note that Jesus, in this discourse with his disciples, is basically addressing the entire Church. To be a church implies, for Matthew, discipleship and imitation of Jesus.[19] Jesus' disciples are paradigmatic figures that allow his readers to be contemporary with Jesus. We have already encountered this feature earlier in the miracle stories. Behind the disciples listening to the Sermon on the Mount, surrounded by a great throng of people, we could discern the Church proclaiming Jesus' commandments to all mankind. And when

---

[17] This interpretation can be found as early as Tertullian (*Fug.* 6,1 = *CChr.SL* 1, 1142). A characteristic example is J. Calvin, *Auslegung der Evangelienharmonie I*, ed. H. Stadtland-Neumann and G. Vogelbusch (Neukirchen-Vluyn: Neukirchener, 1966), 291 and 295–96. Here the ban on travel gear is said to be a quite special Jesuanic instruction rendered possible because, at that time, the disciples were on the road for no more than a few days at a stretch (for short trips it is advisable to travel light!). 'At home they could possess luggage, shoes and additional cloaks, but in order to make them the better fit for travel he ordered them to leave every burden at home.' (*ibid.*, 295–96). Jerome, in his Commentary on Matthew, book IV, 1959 (= *CChr.SL* 77), 65, is able to justify the miraculous healing powers of the apostles (10:8) by pointing out that as uneducated and 'rural' people they had no special need of this authority. Evidently theological training was a latter-day substitute for charisma.

[18] For example by Bornkamm, 'Der Auferstandene' (cf. n. 18, ch. 2), 181–82, and Strecker, *Weg* (cf. n. 18, ch. 1), 196. This type of interpretation is, however, applicable to the Lucan Discourse on Mission, several instructions of which are explicitly retracted by Luke for the later age of the Church (Luke 22:35–36). Luke then goes on to depict Paul (with complete historical justification!) as a fundamentally new type of itinerant radical, albeit he too follows certain instructions from the Mission Discourse (e.g. Acts 13:51).

[19] See Luz, *Matt. II* (cf. n. 8, ch. 4), 154–56.

Jesus now, at the opening of chapter 10, grants authority to his disciples and sends them forth to heal and preach, this too applies to the Church. In essence, Matthew addresses the entire Church as a missionary church, with the disciples partaking of Jesus' authority. They have authority (*exousia*)[20] to cast out evil spirits and to heal 'every kind of ailment and disease' (10:1; cf. 4:23; 9:34). They are told to proclaim the same gospel of the kingdom of heaven as had John the Baptist and Jesus (10:7; cf. 3:2; 4:17). Like Jesus, they are to heal the sick and raise the dead (cf. 9:18–26) and to cleanse lepers (cf. 8:1–4). Not only do they have the same authority as Jesus, they also have the same commission.

With this discourse, according to Matthew, Jesus sends forth his disciples to a fundamentally migrant existence. They are fundamentally 'itinerant radicals'. They share the homelessness of the Son of Man, who has no place where he can lay his head (8:20); they are as poor as Jesus (10:9–10); they enter houses and cities without knowing whether they will be allowed to stay (10:11–13); they roam in Israel from city to city (10:23). On the other hand, quite a large number of logia seem to lose sight of this state of migrancy. Ruptures in families (10:21–22, 34–37), sufferings up to and including martyrdom (10:38–39), interrogations before Sanhedrins and political potentates (10:17–20; cf. 28) – all this may well have primarily affected the preachers of the word (cf. 10:26–27, 32–33; 23:34–35), but it certainly affected others as well. Again and again the discourse transcends the specific conditions of the itinerant radicals. Its conclusion, in verses 40 to 42, is clearly addressed to those members of the community who remain at home, who receive Jesus' itinerant missionaries and grant them hospitality. Evidently both kinds of persons were to be found among the readers of Matthew's Gospel: the itinerant and the sedentary. Among the readers he addresses through his paradigmatic figures, the disciples, Matthew does not distinguish between two fundamentally different groups or classes. Rather,

[20] *Exousia* is a word used by Matthew with particular reference to the authority of Jesus, namely to the limited authority of the earthly Jesus (7:29; 9:6; 21:23ff.) and the unlimited authority of the exalted Lord (28:18; cf. 11:27).

he speaks as if all Christians were itinerant radicals, and yet, at the same time, as if the situation and experiences of the itinerant radicals merely heightened the experiences general to all Christians. One might say that, for Matthew, itinerant radicalism tests the mettle of discipleship. All his readers are, potentially, itinerant radicals. The commission of the itinerant radicals is none other than the commission of the Church altogether. The emphasis on migrancy well accords with Matthew's understanding of the Christian 'way' or 'path' of righteousness. Perhaps he viewed the missionaries, who remain constantly on the move, with neither goods nor protection, proclaiming the kingdom of God, as persons who more closely approached the ideal of Christian perfection (see 19:21). But with the Mission Discourse, rather than having them stand out from the Church, he places them firmly in its centre.[21]

Most striking of all is that Matthew, in his Discourse on Mission, practically never mentions the substance of what Jesus' disciples are to preach but almost exclusively their behaviour and destiny.[22] When he speaks of discipleship (that is, of the Church) he speaks not only of the behaviour of the disciples – their homelessness, poverty (10:9–10) and defencelessness (10:16). Above all he speaks of their destiny: of persecution (10:23) and 'deliverance' to the courts (10:17–18), of family breakdowns and self-preservation (10:29–31), of taking up the cross (10:38), and of death (10:39). Directly or indirectly he gives their experiences a Christological interpretation: their homelessness and poverty is the homelessness and poverty of the follower of Jesus, and hence that of the Son of Man (8:19–20). Their defencelessness is none other than that which Jesus commanded in the Sermon on the Mount

---

[21] Historically, this view implies that the members of the Matthean community were probably not divided into two groups or levels, itinerant and sedentary. Rather, each member was basically summoned to a migrant existence and could become a missionary, including many temporary forms of itinerant radicalism. See U. Luz, 'Die Kirche und ihr Geld im Neuen Testament', in W. Lienemann, ed., *Die Finanzen der Kirche* (Munich: Kaiser, 1989), 535–36.

[22] This is especially important in an ecclesiastical tradition that defines the Church on the basis of its teachings ('word and sacrament') or its institutional form (the 'mystical Body of Christ').

(5:39–42) and which will distinguish his own behaviour in the passion. The first to be 'delivered up' to men was the Son of Man himself (17:22; 20:18; 26:2, 24–25, 45), who has also preceded his followers on the path to the cross and in the sacrifice of his life. In other words, the reason why Matthew finds it so important to speak of the behaviour and destiny of the disciples is that they are images of Jesus himself. Discipleship means conforming to the life of Christ and emulating his model. Matthew has Jesus formulate this in the following words: 'A pupil does not rank above his teacher, or a servant above his master. The pupil should be content to share his teacher's lot, the servant to share his master's. If the master has been called Beelzebub, how much more his household!' (10:24–25). These words are located squarely in the middle of the Mission Discourse, dividing it into two parts. They form the midpoint not only of its text but of its substance.

At the end of our observations on the Sermon on the Mount we noted that the defining property for the Christian-ness of Christians is not words but deeds. The Judge of the world will pass judgment on their 'fruit', that is to say, on their works. At the end of our observations on the Mission Discourse we note that the defining property for the Church is neither confessions of faith nor its institutional fabric, but rather its conformity to Christ. To be a Church means to assume the commission and the authority of Jesus, to live as he did, to suffer as he did. To be a Church means discipleship. To be a Church means itinerancy, movement, commitment and suffering. Taken at its word, Matthew 10 implies that no Church meets the defining qualities of being a Church. But every Church is called upon to do so. Far from providing a *doctrine* of the Church, Matthew says that there is no essence of the Church apart from its practice and its destiny, and hence no possibility of being a Church apart from worldly action and suffering in conformity with its sole exemplar, Jesus.

CHAPTER 5

The origins of the community of disciples in Israel (Matthew 12:1 – 16:20)

JESUS' WITHDRAWALS FROM ISRAEL

Chapter 11 ended with a juxtaposition of opposites: the Galilean cities upon whom Jesus pronounced the judgement of destruction (11:20–24), and the 'simple people' to whom the Father will reveal the things he withholds from the mighty (11:25ff.). In our interpretation this juxtaposition is 'proleptic', or representative of future events. At the moment, the crowds of Israel are still friendly and receptive toward Jesus. The community of those to whom the secret of the Son and the Father is to be revealed has not yet come into existence. Instead, Jesus has healed and taught in Israel. He has called upon disciples there to imitate his way. And he has experienced initial resistance on the part of the scribes and Pharisees. The persecutions and suffering that Jesus announced to his disciples in the Mission Discourse have not yet become a reality, not even for himself.

In the next few chapters the situation comes to a head. Again and again we are given reports of hostility felt toward Jesus by the Jewish leaders. In 12:14 the Pharisees resolve to have him put to death; in 12:24 they accuse him of complicity with the devil. In 12:38 and 16:1 Jesus' Jewish enemies demand a sign. Presumably what they mean in each passage is a cosmic or heavenly sign; simple miracles, which Jesus has, of course, been producing constantly in large quantities, are not enough. In 14:1–12 the scene darkens as Matthew relates the gruesome episode of the death of John the Baptist. This is an interpolation in his Jesus story, a flashback to something that had apparently taken place a short while previously.[1] For Matthew and his readers it is a menacing flashback: verses 14:1–2 reveal that Herod Antipas has also taken notice of Jesus. In 15:1–2 the Pharisees and scribes arrive from Jerusalem. A heated debate ensues.

Jesus repeatedly reacts to such hostility by withdrawing. On three occasions his withdrawal is described with the verb *anachōreō* (12:15, 14:13; 15:21), and once with a different expression (16:4b). Following these withdrawals various things can happen; Matthew's 'plot line' is not very consistent on this point. In 12:15 Jesus withdraws when confronted with the decision of his adversaries to have him put to death. However, the people remain with him as before, and he heals their sick. By 12:24 his enemies, the Pharisees, have reappeared. In 14:13 Jesus withdraws to the desert when he hears of the death of John the Baptist. Again, the people remain with him; he heals them and gives them food. Admittedly the story of the feeding of the multitudes that then follows would have distinctly reminded Matthew's readers of their own experiences in the community, and especially of the Eucharist. The story which follows next, the second calming of the storm, is expressly linked with the disciples. It reaches its climax in the boat with their confession of faith in Jesus' divine sonship (14:33). At that point Jesus' enemies reappear, having arrived from Jerusalem (15:1). The withdrawal that follows upon the ensuing debate (15:21) is probably to Gentile territory, where Jesus remains temporarily in the vicinity of Sidon and Tyre. But this withdrawal is short-lived: soon he is again at the Sea of Galilee, healing and feeding the people. Jesus' sojourn in Gentile territory is thus an exception, as in 8:28–34. Like that earlier passage it anticipates the future. As in 14:14–21, Jesus' withdrawal from his enemies in 15:29–39 is followed by a section depicting his sympathy with and concern for the people, a section transparent of the community's own experience with

---

[1] In 11:2 John is still in prison. In 14:12–13 the news of his murder immediately causes Jesus to withdraw to an isolated spot. Here Matthew forgets that he has already recounted the murder of John as a flashback in 14:1–3. Once again, he is careless in the external trappings of his narrative.

Jesus. The final intervention of Jesus' opponents, their second demand for a sign, is very brief (16:1–2, 4). Here the technique of repetition is at work: the fact that they again demand a sign from heaven, after all that has happened, further underscores their evil. This time Jesus withdraws to his disciples. His concluding instructions to them end with a second confession of faith in Jesus' divine sonship, this time by Peter, and with a forecasting of the new community about to arise, the Church of Jesus.

In its externals, the succession of events is not very coherent. Instead, it functions on a typological level. Again and again the enemies of Jesus make an appearance, incorrigible and evil. Jesus withdraws from them four times. Again and again passages occur that touch on the experiences of the community: a second calming of a storm, two feedings of the multitudes, two confessions of faith in the divine sonship. These repetitions convey an impression that the events are inexorable and fore-ordained. Apparently Jesus can do nothing against the hostility felt toward him; the situation comes increasingly to a head. The community of disciples, for the first time referred to by Jesus as a 'church' (16:18), comes to the fore. Opposite them are the leaders of Israel, who, as the reader becomes increasingly convinced, are evil through and through.

A few more remarks on the leaders of Israel are called for. Those most frequently referred to are the Pharisees, followed by the high priests, the scribes, the elders and the Sadducees. As befits their station, the high priests and the elders play the largest role in Jerusalem, although the Pharisees crop up there as well (see 21:45; 22:34, 41 and 27:62 are redactional). Matthew is fond of having Jesus' enemies appear in groups of two. The combinations are relatively arbitrary: 'scribes and Pharisees' are often found together, or 'high priests and elders' in the story of the passion. But 'Pharisees and Sadducees', 'high priests and scribes' and 'high priests and Pharisees' also occur. In other words Matthew can equally combine people such as the scribes and Pharisees, who had affinities with one another both in history and in the written tradition, or arch-enemies such as the Sadducees and the Pharisees. He is fairly indifferent to what these groups really were and how they related to each other. The only thing that matters to him is that they are all enemies of Jesus. They are given negative traits throughout. Mark was capable of showing a Jewish scribe in a positive light (12:34); Matthew was not.

The preponderance of Pharisees among the ranks of Jesus' enemies is striking. Not only do they occur the most often, the entire Discourse of Woes in chapter 23 is directed at them. The controversy over true purity in Matthew 15 indicates in particular why this is so. The hand-washing scruple is a commandment from Pharisaic circles that did not become general custom until the Pharisees, or at least their successors, had been able to impose the Halakhah on the whole of Israel. Thus, by placing it in the foreground of the conflict, Matthew turns hand-washing into a leading question to reveal which leaders hold power in Israel. Into this pericope Matthew has inserted the phrase 'the blind leading the blind' (verses 12–14). In the Discourse of Woes in chapter 23 the Pharisees are again characterized several times as 'blind leaders' (verses 16, 24). Evidently the Matthean community is struggling against the Pharisees' claims to leadership. This is precisely why they play such a large role among Jesus' enemies.

Between the Jewish leaders and Jesus are the people. They are receptive toward Jesus. Matthew insists upon this time and time again. He can say of the crowds that they 'followed' Jesus (4:25; 8:1; 12:5; 14:13; 19:2). Since *akoloutheō* is a term used by Matthew as a paraphrase for discipleship, the crowds appear in such passages as a potential Church. They are in need of help; the number of accounts of mass healings in Matthew is astonishingly large (12:15; 14:14, 34ff.; 15:29–31). They listen attentively to Jesus (13:1–2). They are always clearly distinguished from the evil leaders of Israel: they consider Jesus to be the Son of David, not an accomplice of the devil (12:23–24). While Herod and his court fear Jesus and seek to have him removed for this reason, the people consider him to be a prophet (21:11, 46; cf. 26:5; 14:5). Matthew is very consistent on this point, and it is actually astonishing how long he sustains a positive picture of the people in his story. Even in Jerusalem he distinguishes quite sharply between the people, who are well-disposed toward Jesus, and their evil leaders (21:15–16, 26, 46). Jesus belongs to the people; he is their Messiah. Not until the very end of the Gospel do the colours suddenly change as the people join the side of their leaders.

On the other hand, our section contains allusions which clearly indicate that, ultimately, even the people will repudiate Jesus. These are found particularly in the announcements of the Judgement, beginning with the proleptic annunciation of the destruction of the Galilean cities in 11:20–24. In the concluding verses of chapter 12 the conflict with the scribes and Pharisees suddenly expands into a conflict with 'this generation', against whom the Queen of Sheba and the Ninevites will appear on the Day of Judgement (12:41–42). The image of the man revisited by evil spirits is a parable for 'this generation' (12:43–45). Above all, however, the Parables Discourse as a whole contrasts Israel's recalcitrance with the understanding of the disciples. This discourse has a special function within the larger context of Matthew 12:1 to 16:20. We shall now look at this function more closely.

JESUS' THIRD DISCOURSE: THE PARABLES DISCOURSE (MATTHEW 13)

The Parables Discourse, which interrupts this main section of the Gospel, falls into two easily discernible parts separated by a break in the narrative. In verse 36 Jesus leaves the crowd that has been listening to him on the shore and enters a house. There the discourse continues, but for the benefit of the disciples alone. This interruption in the story is important as it is in line with the narrative thrust of the entire main section: Jesus' withdrawals into his circle of disciples. The second half of the Parables Discourse is the first of many sets of instructions to the disciples[2] which from now on will be increasingly interspersed in the narrative.

---

[2] See 15:12–20; 16:5–28; 17:9–13, 19–20, 22–23; 17:25 – 18:35; 19:10–12; 19:23 – 20:16; 20:20–8. Actually 13:10–23 is already a set of instructions to the disciples, but Matthew underplays these verses by having Jesus continue speaking to 'them' – i.e.

The correspondences do not end there. The first story, the fourfold parable of the different kinds of soil and its explanation, is interrupted by an interpolation (13:10–17) which Matthew has greatly enlarged from Mark. The point here is that, unlike the disciples, it is not granted to 'those others' to know the secrets of the kingdom of heaven. The eyes of 'this people' look and yet do not see, their ears listen but do not hear or understand. This sets them apart from the disciples, whose eyes and ears are blessed for what they can see and hear beyond the prophets and saints of the Bible (13:13, 16–17). Of 'those others' it is said that even what they now have shall be taken from them.[3] In verses 14–15 Matthew backs up this prediction with a long fulfilment quotation from Isaiah 6:9–10 taken verbatim from the Septuagint – the classical quotation used repeatedly in the New Testament as witness of Israel's recalcitrance.[4] In short, what is being discussed is Israel. The biblical passage itself bears witness to Israel's incomprehensible obstinacy: its lack of understanding, the grossness of its heart, its inability to hear, its eyes shut tight to keep from seeing.[5] When the disciples ask about the meaning of the Parables Discourse spoken to the crowd, their question points to Israel.

At this point, as in 11:16–24 and 12:41–45, today's readers of the Gospel of Matthew will protest and ask why Jesus should speak this way of the people. After all, they are thoroughly well-disposed toward him and have sat patiently on the shore to listen to him. Now they must suffer this treatment at his hands! Since there has always been a tendency to connect 13:10–17 with predestination, modern readers ask why the people of Israel should be dismissed out of hand for no better reason than that their condemnation was pre-ordained by

the people (see verse 34!) – without any particular comment. Not until verse 36 is the change of listeners stressed. It is then clearly maintained to the end of the discourse (13:52!)

[3] This verse will be taken up and continued in 21:43: the *basileia* shall be taken from them.

[4] See Mark 4:12, John 12:40 and Acts 28:26–27.

[5] *Mēpote* ... in 13:15, rather than referring to divine predestination, puts on record Israel's guilt: they closed their ears and eyes so as not to hear or see, otherwise God would truly heal them! Regarding this interpretation see Luz, *Matt. II* (cf. n. 8, ch. 4), 314.

divine decree in Isaiah. Whatever the case, this was not Matthew's view of the matter. To understand him we must remember that all the discourses in Matthew are 'spoken to the winds', directly addressing contemporary readers of his Gospel. *They* know that the great majority of the people of Israel repudiated the words of Jesus. They, as well as large parts of the primitive Church, interpret this knowledge, gained in their own present day, in the light of Isaiah 6:9–10. At the same time, drawing on their own experiences and recalling passages such as 2:3–4, 8:10–13, 11:7–24 and 12:38–45, they sense that Israel's repudiation will form the end of Matthew's story of Jesus. In other words, they read Jesus' discourse from their own contemporary vantage point. This vantage point, though, is not part of Matthew's narrative thread. On the contrary, it breaks that thread, or at times tightens it, thereby focusing attention on the final denouement. By keeping the future in mind, it helps readers to understand, and to interpret, what is brewing in the Gospel and what Matthew has to tell them, both before and after chapter 13.

Accordingly, Matthew's Parables Discourse has a 'salvational' dimension related to the history of mankind's salvation. However, this does not only apply to the discourse in its totality, but also to individual parables. Regarding the four kinds of soil, we would have to say that the well-trodden ground on the footpath stands for the fate of Jesus' teachings in Israel. In other parables the salvational dimension is even clearer and more explicit. The parable of the weeds is said, by Matthew in 13:37–43, to relate to the coexistence of the righteous and the unrighteous in the world until the judgement of the Son of Man. The parable of the net is given a similar interpretation (13:49–50). In his instruction of the disciples, then, Jesus enlarges the perspective to the end of history, to the Last Judgement. Even the parables of the mustard seed and the leaven (13:31–33), which Matthew leaves unexplained, are presumably intended in his view to be given an allegorical interpretation. Following upon the parable of the weeds, which dealt with the experience of evil in the community, these two parables have the purpose of imparting courage. Once again Jesus speaks of a sower (readers will naturally think of Jesus himself) who sows one tiny seed. This tiny seed is promised a glorious future. It is my assumption that in this parable Matthew and his community (unlike the original narrator, Jesus, who was speaking of God's kingdom) were thinking of their own tiny church. The birds nesting in the mustard shrub may perhaps have meant to them the promise attendant upon the Gentile mission, on which they had now been sent by the risen Lord. It may be that the ecclesiological interpretation of these parables – an interpretation that later came to prevail in the Church – already had its roots in Matthew. However, we must bear in mind that Matthew was relating these passages to a small and oppressed minority community. Later, a Church triumphant in the temporal world would use the ecclesiological interpretations of these passages to reinforce its own feeling of triumph.

Even outside the Parables Discourse, Matthew's Gospel has parables that cry out for a salvational interpretation. Here I would like to recall, as representative examples, the parable of the children at play (11:16–19), the passage on the evil spirits revisiting the body, raised by Matthew to the level of a parable (12:43–45), and especially the great trilogy of parables in 21:28 to 22:14: the two sons, the vineyard and the marriage feast.[6] Rhetorical means for giving a salvational interpretation to these parables were offered to Matthew by the device of allegory.[7] In some cases he could take advantage of a large number of traditional metaphors already operative in these parables: seed/word, harvest/judgement, king/God, and others. Such metaphors could project their meanings more easily in surroundings where they were readily understood without further explanation.

Besides the salvational interpretation, the 'parenetical' or exhortatory interpretation of parables was also important to Matthew. In the Parables Discourse this can be seen at work in

---

[6] See pp. 118–120 below.
[7] By 'allegory' I do not mean a literary genre but rather a rhetorical figure (see Quintilian, *Inst. Orat.* 8,6,44) in which the literal and figurative meanings are distinct. This device may be found in various genres, including that of parable.

the very first example, the fourfold parable of the different kinds of soil (13:3–23). The pre-Marcan community had already applied this parable parenetically to the different kinds of people who hear the word of God.[8] In this instance, then, Matthew was following the tradition of his sources. The important point is that, after the blessing of the disciples, no distinction is made between listeners inside and outside the community. Even within the community it is apparently possible for members, following their initial enthusiasm and joy, to relapse into states of need and persecution, or to be crushed by cares or the lure of money. To belong to the community is not tantamount to bearing fruit.

Thereafter, in the second part of the chapter, all the parables have a dominant parenetical component. This dimension is evidently of special importance in those parables spoken to the disciples in the instruction on faith and practice. The explanation of the parable of the weeds in the wheat field in 13:37–43 focuses on the denouement, on the judgement of the Son of Man. So does the conclusion of the parable of the net in 13:49–50. The preceding catalogue of allegorical explanations in verses 37 to 39 merely has the function of preparing this conclusion. Here, too, Matthew does not distinguish between the Church and the world. The field on which the Son of Man has sown the good seed is the world; in the world, wheat and weeds grow together and intermingle. Surely the crucial experience for Matthew is the experience of evil within his community.[9] Far from being 'pure', his community resembles the world. Both the wheat field (13:38) and the kingdom of the Son of Man (13:41) are the world. The explanation of the parable directs an appeal to *all* persons, both inside and outside the community, to be wheat and not weeds. The imagery is inconsistent on this point: neither wheat nor weeds can change

---

[8] To my mind this was always the meaning of the fourfold parable – not so much a single parable as a series of four parallel parables on the same subject. See Luz, *Matt. II* (cf. n. 90), 308–11.

[9] The same can be said of the pre-Matthean community that 'paraphrased' the Marcan parable of the self-germinating seed (Mark 4:26–29) to form the parable of the weeds. It must have realized that the seed of God's kingdom evidently will not grow 'automatically'. The enemy will sow bad seed while the farmer sleeps.

their nature. But this is not so in the interpretation, where wheat stands for the 'righteous', and weeds for the *skandala*[10] and the perpetrators of *anomia* ('lawlessness'). By 'lawlessness' we should understand everything that contradicts the biblical Law newly proclaimed by Jesus, first and foremost the commandment of love. But when all men feel equally called upon to perform acts of righteousness and love, what special quality will the community then have that makes it superior to the world? Reading between the lines of this passage, we would have to say that the special quality resides merely in the fact that the community *hears* the word and *knows* what it means – that its members have Jesus as their teacher, who instructs them until they have comprehended everything of prime importance. The advantage of the disciples lies merely in the fact that they have understood what it is all about (13:51). In this way our text, without speaking explicitly of the Church, contains an ecclesiological concept that will occupy us later.

Other Matthean parables must also be given parenetical interpretations. In the Parables Discourse, to my way of thinking, the two parables of the hidden treasure and the pearl (13:44–46) attempt to draw attention to the need to renounce possessions for the sake of the kingdom of God. In both parables the emphasis lies on the phrase 'he sold everything he had'. Later the story of the wealthy man (19:21) will elucidate the meaning of these two parables within the larger context of the Gospel. Other parenetical parables include most of those which Matthew has Jesus say to the disciples at the end of the story, following the great reckoning with Israel (24:45 – 25:30). They confront his readers, or his listeners, with the final great alternative. Faced with the Last Judgement, they find themselves in an either-or situation. Usually the parables only state indirectly how this alternative becomes concrete. They may, for example, be bracketed by the word 'awake' (24:42; 25:13). In the parable of the housebuilders this is done by referring back to the entire Sermon on the Mount with the phrase 'act upon my words' (7:24–27), in the parable of the two servants

---

[10] Persons who are a 'cause of stumbling'; see 18:6–7. The expression shows just how closely Matthew drew in effect on the experiences of his community.

by having the bad servant eat and drink and bully his fellow servants (24:49). What is also evident in these judgement parables is that the parenetic interpretation does not exclude the salvational: the moment a parable begins to touch upon the Judgement it automatically takes on a salvational dimension.

Thus, in the Matthean parables, salvational and parenetic interpretations generally stand alongside and complement each other. The allegories and traditional metaphors contained within them serve both ends. Matthew's understanding of the parables thus proves to be a bridge to the way they were understood by the Old Church. There, of course, as a result of the many-layered meaning of the Scripture, the parables were given not only 'mystical' (allegorical and salvational) but also 'tropological' (ethical) interpretations. Both interpretative possibilities coexisted as different but not opposing potential meanings of the texts. Both seem to be present in embryo in Matthew's explanations of the parables. I would even go farther and maintain that both have their roots in Jesus. In Jesus' parables we find, again and again, that his own works and his mission to Israel are mirrored in parabolic form, for example in the parable of the invitation to the great feast, or that of the mustard seed. Herein lies the germ-cell for their later salvational interpretation. But we also discover, again and again, that Jesus' parables are not simply meant to be theoretical. Their significance points again and again to everyday life: they ask to be lived, not to be grasped by the intellect. Herein lie the roots of their later parenetic interpretation. In sum, I do not view the rift between Jesus' parables and their later exegesis by the Church as an unbridgeable chasm.[11] Indeed, I see Matthew as a bridge between them.

THE CHURCH IN ISRAEL

In the vehement controversies with Israel's leaders we begin to discern, with growing clarity, the image of a community of

---

[11] As has been assumed ever since A. Jülicher, *Die Gleichnisreden Jesu I* (Tübingen: Mohr, 1910²).

disciples standing opposed to the hostile portion of Israel under the leadership of the Pharisees and scribes. This community is the Church nascent in Israel. It is spoken of in many ways: first in texts dealing with the disciples and reflecting the experiences of the Church, and again in those sayings of Jesus that touch upon the Church.

(1) As we have seen,[12] the disciples are paradigmatic for, or representative of, the Matthean community. The chapters we are discussing show Jesus as the teacher of his disciples, and thus the Church in a process of learning. In the middle of the Parables Discourse Jesus abandons the crowd listening to him on the shore and enters the house with his disciples (13:36), where he resumes his instruction for their benefit alone. At the end of his narratives and explanations he asks them, 'Have you understood all this?' (13:51). Obviously he wants the disciples to understand his instructions. This explains why, in the next sections of his story, Jesus continually interweaves special instructions to the disciples to aid them in their comprehension (e.g. 15:12–20; 16:5–12, 13–28; 17:10–13, 19–20; 17:25 – 18:35). On several occasions Matthew explicitly states that the disciples have understood (16:12; 17:23). He declined to adopt, from his Marcan source, the lack of understanding from the disciples that plays such a large role in the parallel section of Mark's Gospel. For Matthew the disciples, though capable of comprehending, are not yet at the point of comprehension. They require instruction from their teacher, Jesus.

The community of disciples emerging in Israel, then, is a learning community. Why is this so important to Matthew? An answer to this question may be found in his explanation of the fourfold parable of the types of soil. Only of the fourth type of listeners, with whom the word has fallen on fertile ground, does Matthew claim that they 'hear and understand the word' (13:23). The word, once understood, bears fruit. For Matthew, then, understanding is associated with the bearing of fruit. At the first level this doubtless refers to an intellectual process: there are parables or riddles, such as 13:24–30, 15:11 and 16:6,

---

[12] Cf. pp. 75–80 and 86 above.

which Jesus must explain. But the fourfold parable of the soil shows that understanding is not just an intellectual act. Here the disciples do not simply grasp something after hearing Jesus' explanation. Here understanding is something more than an act of intellect: it means realizing what a word signifies to oneself, holding on to that realization, and putting it into practice. This is why, to Matthew's way of thinking, those who let go of the word after their initial enthusiasm have not understood it. Understanding goes hand in hand with the bearing of fruit, and it is this fruit that ultimately matters. This explains why the 'understanding' of the disciples, and the associated, highly pragmatic instruction of their teacher, Jesus, are so important for the Church.

But the Church is not only a learning community. It is also a community for the imparting and sharing of experience. It is the place where the powerful presence of Jesus can be felt. At this point we must return to the miracle stories. It is no coincidence that the section we are discussing contains several miracle stories symbolizing ecclesial experiences. These include the two stories of the feeding of the multitudes (14:13–21; 15:32–39), behind which the readers and listeners of Matthew's Gospel can visualize the experience of Communion and perhaps even the 'love feasts' (*agapē*) and solicitude of the community. They also include the second calming of the storm (14:22–33), which Matthew has adorned with the episode of the drowning Peter. The ecclesial character of this story is evident above all in its conclusion, where the disciples cast themselves upon the ground (a strange thing to do in a rocking boat!) and pay homage to Jesus, proclaiming their faith in him with the classic words of the congregational confession: 'Truly you are the Son of God.' Before then we are told the story of the drowning Peter. Though able to walk on water, Peter is seized with fear as he looks at the storm and begins to sink beneath the waves. As in 8:25 his cry, 'Save me, Lord!', is taken from the community's prayer of supplication. The protective hand held out by Jesus recalls the language of the Bible; the community is 'in God's hand'. The experience encountered by Peter in his prayer is once again characterized as 'little faith'. Faith is mingled with doubt (see also 28:17). Faith is expressed in prayer. Prayer is a cry for God's help, at once encompassing trust and desperation. Faith, for Matthew, is not simply a permanent possession, the self-assurance of a man who knows that his game is won.

In his addendum in 14:28–31 Matthew has represented, in the figure of the drowning Peter, an experience fundamental to every disciple of Jesus. Here Peter has become the archetypal disciple. In Matthew's Gospel he plays a larger role than any of the other disciples. Again and again he is made to stand for experiences and situations typical of discipleship. Peter is the one who asks for or receives instruction from Jesus the teacher (see, for example, 15:15; 18:21; 19:27–30; 26:33–34). He represents the disciples' proximity to Christ and yet, at the same time, their frailty. It is he who denies Jesus with an oath and then repents (26:69–75). It is he who is unable to hold vigil (26:37, 40). He puts his faith to the test – and sinks (14:28–31). He proclaims his faith in the Son of God – and shuns suffering. He is the 'Rock' – and 'Satan' (16:16, 22).

Peter is the typical disciple, and at the same time the most important of them. Why is he so important? There are several reasons. He was the first to be called (4:18–20; 10:2). He was with Jesus from the very beginning. After Easter he played a decisive role in the larger body of the Church as the most important of Jesus' disciples. Unlike the other leading figures of primitive Christianity, in particular Paul and James the Lord's brother, he was Jesus' own disciple. His role as the leading apostle and foremost figure in the post-apostolic period, precedent over Paul and James, is thoroughly in keeping with the fundamental importance of the Jesus tradition in the post-apostolic Church. During the post-apostolic period Peter was the principal figure of the Church for the simple reason that the *kyrios* ('lord'), the living word of Jesus, was the Church's primary authority. For the Church, the figure of Peter embodies a reminder that it is indissolubly bound to Jesus as its origin and foundation. It is precisely for this reason that Matthew could make Peter the leading typical disciple.

Thus, the figure of Peter unites the unique and the typical.

For Matthew, to be a disciple, and to be a church, means *continually* to be bound to the *unique* historical figure of Jesus. It means continually to learn from and be encouraged by him, continually to gain experiences of faith with him who is at once the living Jesus, and to receive forgiveness over and over again from him and from no other.[13]

(2) At the end of the first main section, in the significant passage 11:25–30, Jesus contrasts the community of disciples for the first time with Israel, now under judgement. According to the traditional verses 25–27 the community belongs to the *nēpioi* – the 'simple ones' – as opposed to Israel's religious and intellectual elite. The word *nēpioi* has connotations of naive, uneducated, slow-witted. Here Jesus was thinking of his listeners: the women, the poor, the simple folk of Galilee, none of whom had a chance to obtain learning from the 'sages'. Here Matthew was thinking of the Church: they are the 'simple ones'. Later, in 18:1–9, he will place the 'little people' firmly at the centre of his community. It is they, and not the sages of Israel, to whom the revelation of the Son is given.

To verses 25–27 Matthew appends a proverb in verses 28–30, a promise of relief for the hard-working and heavy-laden. To Matthew, if we are to judge from 23:4, the 'heavy-laden' may well refer to those who had been given heavy burdens by the teachers of Israel. The 'hard-working' are almost certainly not the 'weary', as they are called in Luther's German translation (*Mühseligen*), but those who exert themselves.[14] They are permitted to learn from Jesus that[15] he is kind and humble of heart. This proverb thus unites the promise of salvation with an imperative element. The 'simple ones' are promised peace and the easy yoke of him who, unlike the Pharisees (23:4),

---

[13] Further thoughts on Matthew's portrayal of Peter can be found in R. Brown, K. P. Donfried and J. Reumann, *Peter in the New Testament* (Minneapolis: Paulist, 1972), 83–101, and P. Hoffmann, 'Die Bedeutung des Petrus für die Kirche des Matthäus', in J. Ratzinger, ed., *Dienst an der Einheit* (Düsseldorf: Patmos, 1978), 9–26.

[14] See Wisd. of Sol. 6:14, 9:10 and 10:17, Ecclus. 24:34 and 33:18, and Matthew 6:28.

[15] Usually *hoti* is translated as 'because'. As in other passages such as 24:32, however, I tend to agree with Strecker (cf. n. 18, ch. 1), 174, and translate it as 'that'. The disciples are meant to learn from Jesus, both in theory and in practice, *that* he is kind and humble.

actually enacted the very qualities he demands from them: kindness, humility and love. But the promise of salvation is conditioned by human activity. Blessed are those who learn – and who exert themselves!

Matthew proceeds here in much the same way as in the Beatitudes of 5:3–12. The open, unlimited promise of salvation given to the poor, the suffering and the uneducated is linked to the Church and comes to fulfilment within the Church. It is those members of the community who suffer for Jesus' sake (5:11–12) who are called blessed. But their unrestricted blessing is combined with an ethical element. Blessed are those who are kind (5:5; cf. 11:29), or who exert themselves, perhaps in the cause of righteousness (11:28; cf. 5:6). Blessed are the men and women of peace, the pure of heart and the merciful (5:7–9). Now that the doctrine of divine grace had been preached for half a century, it is important for Matthew to say that salvation can also be put to the test. This explains why, in 11:25–30, the 'simple ones' are also those who exert themselves. The attainment of grace through obedience – human activity – becomes a significant feature of the community of disciples.

Precisely this point is expressed at the end of chapter 12 in the second important passage on the disciples, whom Matthew contrasts with 'this generation' of Israel (12:45). It is the passage dealing with Jesus' 'true relatives', adopted from the Gospel of Mark (12:46–50). There Jesus' 'true relatives' were those who did God's will. Into this text Matthew has interpolated a brief clause that reads 'holding out his hand over the disciples' (verse 49a). In this way he transforms the Marcan text into something akin to a 'definition'[16] of true discipleship, and hence of the Church. The Church are those who perform the will of the Father. It is they who stand under the protective hand of Jesus (see 14:31).

The final passage on the disciples in the main section we are discussing is the story of Peter's confession in 16:13–20. Not only the first main section of 4:23 to 11:30, but also the second from 12:1 to 16:20, ends with a forward glance to the Church.

[16] Trilling, *Das wahre Israel* (cf. n. 18, ch. 1), 30.

Here the word 'church' occurs for the first time in Matthew's Gospel. In this way Matthew explicitly states what the community of disciples emerging in Israel actually is. It has a new name – 'my "congregation"', as distinct from the old 'congregation', Israel. In so doing Matthew supplies a catchword for the matters he wishes to relate in the next main section from 16:21 to 20:34. In this text Peter, once again, appears as the typical disciple. He confesses his faith in Jesus as the Son of God, as all the disciples had done before in 14:33. And Jesus gives him his blessing, as he had done before to all the disciples in 13:16–17. Peter receives the commission to 'bind and loose', presumably to teach with full authority in the name of Jesus, as all the disciples are enjoined to do in 18:18. And confronted with the reality of suffering he recoils and turns from a Rock into a Satan (16:21–23), much as all the disciples were to do later (cf. 18:1; 26:56). When Jesus calls Peter a 'Rock', the foundation of the building or temple that is the Church,[17] it is not because of his personal qualities, or because he is in advance of the other disciples. Rather, Peter is given this epithet because he is the first and, for the Church, most significant disciple *of Jesus*. Without a permanent link to Jesus and his teachings the Church could not be what it is.[18]

THE DISCIPLES' CONFESSION OF FAITH IN THE SON
OF GOD

In the two texts, both dealing with the Church, that conclude the first and second main sections of the Gospel the title 'Son of God' plays a decisive role. For Matthew it seems to conceal the central core of faith, of God's revelation and the confession of

[17] Cf. Gal. 2:9, 1 Cor. 3:9–17, Eph. 2:20–2.
[18] Objectively speaking, this means that the exegetically false interpretations of the 'Rock' by Augustine (as referring to *Christ*) and the Orthodox Church's (the faith of the Church) are therefore closer to Matthew's original meaning than later Roman Catholic attempts to construct a permanent legal primacy for Peter's successors on the basis of his personal function as a rock or foundation. In the larger body of the Church this 'Roman' interpretation stood very much on the sidelines until the time of the Counter-Reformation. Only in reaction to the Reformation did it become the official Catholic exegesis. See U. Luz, 'Das Primatwort Matthäus 16,17–19 aus wirkungsgeschichtlicher Sicht', *N.T.S*, 37 (1991), 415–33.

the community. This expression was already significant in the
Prologue to the Gospel.[19] There two things became clear. First,
'Son of God' refers to God's revelation of the secret of Christ,
a secret residing in Jesus' divine lineage (1:18–25) and the
messianic authority invested in him by God (3:16–17). Only
God himself could have made this secret known to Jesus.
Second, however, Matthew emphasizes the obedience of the
Son of God (3:15; 4:1–11; cf. 27:43, 54). Jesus' divine sonship
involves not only the secret of his divine origins but also the fact
that he constitutes a model on which the faithful can pattern
their lives. For Matthew, then, the divine sonship has both a
'vertical' and a 'horizontal' dimension.

Both of these dimensions in turn appear in three key passages: 11:25–30, 16:13–28 and, in the next main section of the
Gospel, 17:1–13. The first of these opens in 11:25–27 with a
prayer from Jesus to his Father. In this prayer, in the con-
fidential relation between Father and Son, Jesus discloses part
of his secret: 'Everything is entrusted to me' (11:27). On the
basis of 4:8–10 and 28:18 one might at first think of this phrase
as referring to the power that the exalted Lord holds over
heaven and earth. In the context of 11:25–26, however, one
tends instead to think of the revelation granted to the Son. This
is how it is elaborated in verse 27: the Son[20] knows the Father,
and the Father knows the Son. This mutual 'knowledge' is
exclusive: no one but the Son knows the Father, and no one but
the Father knows the secret of the Son. It is also 'symmetrical'[21]
in that both Father and Son stand on the same plane in a
reciprocal relation of 'cognizance'. The wording recalls the
writings of the mystics on the divine correlative, except that in
this case it is Jesus alone who is correlated to God in 'mystical'
awareness. On the basis of our text one might say that the
unique aspect of the 'Son' is that he belongs to the Father. This

---

[19] See pp. 35–37 above.

[20] In the context of Matthew's Gospel 'Son' naturally has the same meaning as 'Son of
God', notwithstanding all the many (and to my mind arduous!) attempts to
postulate a special 'son Christology' for the pre-Matthean tradition.

[21] The verb applied both to Father and Son – *epignoskein* – precludes an 'asymmetrical'
interpretation in which, say, the Father 'chooses' the Son and the Son 'acknowledges' the Father.

explains why the Son of God cannot be revealed to Peter by a mortal man, but only by the Father alone (16:17). It also explains why, on the mountain of transfiguration, a heavenly voice proclaims this crucial realization a second time to the disciples – and to the readers of the Gospel (17:5). Matthew, in other words, is fully aware of a Christology 'from above' even though he is writing a gospel with a strong ethical bias and is keenly interested in Jesus as a teacher and exemplar.

At this point, however, the vertical dimension of faith is joined by the horizontal. As Matthew would have preferred to put it, the revealed divine sonship of Jesus assumes concrete form in life. Verses 11:25–27, after all, do not rest content with the revelation of Jesus' divine sonship, which is then, in a second stage, to be revealed by the Son to the 'simple ones', the community. Rather, the 'Son' is at the same time one who is 'kind and humble', a servant rather than a master of humanity (20:28). That the Son is revealed to the elect – the simple ones – does not mean that they participate like disembodied spirits in the extraordinary, mystically reciprocal awareness between Father and Son, but rather that they 'learn' from Jesus to travel a very specific path. The awareness of the Son is connected with obedience.

This same realization is in turn expressed in the next passage on the divine sonship in 16:13–28. The important point here is that 16:13–20 is given a continuation in 16:21–28.[22] Peter's confession of faith in Jesus' divine sonship must prove its worth in everyday life. This life is the path of suffering which Jesus, the Son of Man, must now travel. The recognition of Christ 'from above' is now drawn down into lowliness. The recognition of the divine sonship is but one step on the path of the imitation of Jesus' passion; it cannot be achieved without self-denial, suffering and martyrdom. Finally the last text, 17:2–13, reveals the same structure once again. We shall see

---

[22] The two texts stand in a 'chiastic' or mirror relation. On the outside are the instructions to the disciples, with a statement of the divine sonship (verses 13–15, 24–28). These flank conversations with Peter in which the disciple is directly addressed in the second person (Rock – Satan) and the divine and the human appear as opposites (verses 16–9, 22–23.). In the middle are Jesus's instructions to the disciples (verses 20, 21).

that the ascent of the mountain necessarily entails a descent from that same mountain, that knowledge from above necessarily entails a path far below.[23]

The vertical and the horizontal, revealed knowledge and worldly obedience, mysticism and everyday life: for Matthew these things all coalesce. There is a path leading directly from Matthew to the later ecclesial Christology of the dual nature of Christ, as surprising as this may seem at first glance, and as little as Matthew himself may have thought in terms of natures or substances.

[23] See pp. 103–4 below.

CHAPTER 6

The life of the community of disciples
(Matthew 16:21 – 20:34)

THE PATH FROM THE MOUNTAIN TO THE VALLEY

The main section that now follows in our Gospel focuses on the community of disciples and the regulation of their lives. For this section Matthew turned to and expanded upon Mark 8:27 to 10:52. In Mark's Gospel the section is articulated primarily by the three announcements of the passion of the Son of Man in 8:31, 9:31 and 10:32–34. These correspond in Matthew to 16:21, 17:22–23 and 20:17–19. In Matthew's version, however, the symmetry of Mark's design has been somewhat upset by the interpolation of new material. By recasting the Discourse on Community in chapter 18[1] and inserting the extensive parable of the workers in the vineyard (20:1–16) Matthew has made the section between the second and third announcements of the passion (17:24 – 20:16) roughly three times as long as that between the first two. As a result, this middle section deals almost exclusively with questions of the life of the community of disciples – questions that have little or nothing to do with their suffering – while the subject of suffering is placed centre stage at the beginning (16:21 – 17:23) and the end (20:17–34). The result for the entire main section is a three-part structure superimposed upon the formal layout of narrative – discourse – narrative.

On the surface, we notice that in this section Jesus' con-

---

[1] This discourse, like most of the other discourses, draws on Marcan material (18:1–9 = Mark 9:33–50) and is made up of special sayings from 18:10 onwards. As in the Sermon on the Mount, Matthean special sayings (18:10, 12–13, 15b–18, 19–20) are complemented by material from Q (18:15a, 22–23).

troversies with his opponents, which dominated the preceding
main section, now recede completely into the background. It is
as though we had suddenly entered an area free of wind and
storm, the 'eye of the hurricane'.[2] The people likewise decrease
in importance.[3] The action now takes place between Jesus and
his circle of disciples. Instructions to the disciples (17:9–13,
19–20, 22–23; 17:25 – 18:35; 19:10–12; 19:23 – 20:16;
20:20–28) and stories of the disciples (17:1–8, 14–18; 19:13–22)
predominate.

Standing at the very outset of this main section is the first
announcement of the passion of the Son of Man (16:21). The
label 'Satan' hurled at Peter fetches the confessor back to the
bright glare of reality. The passages that now follow, dealing
with the imitation of the passion and the renunciation of life
(16:24–25), are repeated from 10:38f. Readers are already
familiar with them and can take them all the more readily to
heart. Suffering, for Matthew, is not a matter of passive
acquiescence but an active principle of life ('If anyone wishes
to be a follower of mine . . .'). 'Self-denial' does not simply
mean ascetic self-castigation; rather, it is the obverse side of the
'confession' of faith in Christ and must be understood from that
vantage point (see esp. 26:69–75). The point is not a longing
for martyrdom per se so much as a 'way' or 'path'. The
affirmation of Christ sets the believer on a path that may,
perhaps, end in martyrdom.[4] From 10:24–25 and 16:21 it
clearly transpires that this path to suffering is the path of
conformity to Christ. The servant must be content to share his
master's lot! Suffering, Matthew tells us, cannot be avoided
when one chooses to travel the way of Christ and to take his
radical commands at their full value. To say 'no' to oneself is
the natural consequence of saying 'yes' to Christ. But Matthew
does not spell out what that suffering will be, just as in 5:20 he

---

[2] Only in 19:3 do the Pharisees make an appearance, but without producing a
controversy.

[3] They appear as an active force only in 19:2 and 20:29–31; cf. their role in 17:14.

[4] Martyrdom is specifically mentioned in 10:39 and 16:25. Still, 'taking up the cross'
automatically suggests the path a condemned man is forced to travel en route to his
execution, having taken up the cross at the outset. It is therefore only fitting that
10:38 should be followed by 10:39, and 16:24 by 16:25.

leaves undefined the minimum amount of superior righteousness acceptable to the Son of Man. Consequently, martyrdom need not be a defining feature of the Christian life,
although it may become one. An evasion of suffering, as
demonstrated on several occasions by Peter and, later, by the
other disciples (16:22; 18:1; 20:20–21; 26:56, 69–70), is in-
compatible with discipleship and contradicts the profession of
faith in the Son of God – a profession which is not simply
directed 'upward'.

Religious experience and the passion are impressively inter-
twined in Matthew's story of the transfiguration. The story
falls into two parts, the actual transfiguration (17:1–8) and the
discussion with the disciples (17:10–13), with verse 9 functioning as a sort of hinge. In the transfiguration itself the voice of
God (verse 5–6) forms the central core, with the remaining
verses arranged around it in concentric rings, a rhetorical
device known as 'chiasmus'. Jesus with Elijah and Moses (verses
2–4) and Jesus alone (verses 7–8) are flanked on either side by
the ascent and descent of the mountain (verses 1 and 9). *Christo-
logically*, the principal concerns are, first of all, the revelation of
the Son of God, the immersion of Jesus in the celestial realm of
which he shall become Lord, and a premonition of the future
grandeur and nobility of him whom God has already proclaimed to be his Son (3:17) and to whom all power over
heaven and earth shall be given (11:27; 28:18). But the transfiguration is equally concerned with Jesus' path as the Son of
Man, a path leading to suffering and death. The disciples
already know that the Baptist is the foreordained Elijah (11:10,
14), and they 'understand' what Jesus is saying to them.
Ecclesiologically, it is significant that by expanding verses 6–8
and connecting them more closely with verses 10–13 Matthew
has channelled his narrative in the direction of a disciple story.
On the one hand he wishes to present a particular religious
experience of the disciples at a particular location in anticipation of the glory of Easter. Great leeway is given to the readers'
powers of association; all manner of ideas, memories of their
own worship and mystical experiences may attach themselves
to this story. Matthew's concern is to present, literally, a 'peak

experience', unique and unreduplicatable, perhaps even mystical, and to partake of the divine majesty. The disciples are with Jesus on the mountaintop as fellow participants with their own religious 'peak experiences' and, at the same time, with their incomprehension.

Another point of the story, however, is to reveal the limits of such experiences and to prepare for the return to ordinary life. Experiences of this sort are not meant to be prolonged indefinitely in some sort of 'retreat'; the touch of the divine hand casts man to the ground and makes him speechless. And it is in this condition that the disciples encounter Jesus without a heavenly retinue, 'alone' (verse 8), speaking to them, dispelling their fears, touching them and causing them to rise up. This, too, is an experience of divinity, and to Matthew it is an important one. The same Jesus, 'alone', takes the disciples with him as he descends from the high mountain to the plain, where all that awaits them is the path of suffering. The path to the glory of Easter, foreshadowed on the mountaintop, thus leads through the plain – and to suffering. In terms of Christology, what this means is that the Son of God, resurrected and apotheosized, and the Son of Man, travelling his earthly path to suffering, remain inseparable. For the disciples, what this means is that the only persons who can truly understand are those who partake of both – the peak religious experience and the path of suffering. Without the latter, overpowering religious experiences become illusory or bring men and women merely fear and speechlessness. Conversely, without overwhelming religious experiences, the path to suffering becomes a funeral dirge devoid of hope.

CHURCH DISCIPLINE AND RULES OF FORGIVENESS
(MATTHEW 18)

A peculiar tension pervades the Discourse on the Community in Matthew 18. At its centre, in verses 15 to 17, is the rule of excommunication. It deals with the expulsion of sinners from the community following a discussion, first in private, then with one or two listeners, and finally before the assembled community. Such regulations are familiar to us from other sources, for example from Qumran (1 *QS* 6:1–2; *CD* 9:2–4). This is how things must be done in a community that wishes to make manifest its own sacredness. The Qumran community was such a community. So is Matthew's.

Viewed from a sociological standpoint, the Matthean community has many structural elements in common with a sect visibly in the process of self-definition.[5] Like the 'sect rule' in the Qumran community, the Law as interpreted by Jesus functions as a 'rule' which, by self-definition, is mandatory for the community and allows it to separate the 'sinners' from its other members. It is a community that distinguishes itself from other Jews by its 'superior righteousness' and whose defining feature is obedience. A community of this sort will attempt, at least in outline, to draw boundaries between itself and others. We also know that the evil in its midst posed a problem to the Matthean community (see 13:24–30; 22:10). This problem is solved by the process of excommunication described in 18:15–18. Characteristically, the Matthean community has no official empowered to warn or expel sinners.[6] On the contrary, excommunication is the task of all the brethren; the final arbiter, rather than being vested in a bishop or court of law, was the assembled community itself. This is fully consistent with the fraternal church structure we encounter in, for example, 23:8–10: 'You have one teacher and all of you are brothers.' Such 'offices' as existed in the Matthean church – scribe, teacher, prophet – were integrated into this fraternal structure. In short, I assume that the 'rule of excommunication' in Matthew 18:15–18 reflected actual conditions in the Matthean church.

---

[5] I define 'sect' as does M. Weber in *Wirtschaft und Gesellschaft* (Tübingen: Mohr, 1980), 721–22: 'an association ... based on free agreement among its members and consisting', unlike a church, 'of persons with full religious qualifications. At times it even forms an *ecclesia pura* ... the visible community of saints from whose midst the black sheep are expunged.'

[6] Kilpatrick, *Matthew* (cf. n. 1, ch. 1), 79, assumes without justification that the discourse is directed at the community's leaders. In fact, this does not occur until the *Didaskalia* of Pseudo-Matthew (10 = 2:38), where excommunication is the responsibility of bishops and deacons.

This assumption is strengthened by the tradition from which the Matthean community arose. The emissaries of Jesus in the Sayings Source, who probably belong to the prehistory of the Matthean community, represented the authority of their Lord: whoever receives them receives Jesus, and whoever receives Jesus receives God (10:40). Whoever rejects them, however, incurs the Judgement, as one sign of which the rejected emissaries shake the dust from their feet (10:14). To repudiate their claim altogether is apparently a sin against the Holy Spirit, a sin which is unforgivable (12:32). This is consistent with the authority of Jesus' disciples to 'bind and loose', that is, to make decisions of doctrine and to forgive or condemn sins (18:18; cf. 16:19). This logion was probably appended to the rule of excommunication prior to Matthew in order to legitimize the community's authority.[7] Thus, even in its earlier traditions the Matthean community had sectarian and elitist traits.

There thus arises a quite peculiar tension between the centre of the chapter and the surrounding texts. This tension is glaringly evident in 18:21–22: 'seventy times seven' is Jesus' answer to Peter's question about the number of times one should forgive, far outstripping the 'seven times a day' given by the Sayings Source. The passage seems to imply that there are no tangible limits to forgiveness. This is also the gist of the parable of the lost sheep in 18:12–14. Matthew departs from tradition in his interpretation of this parable. Rather than associating it with God and his relation to sinners, Matthew relates it to the community. Christians should strive under all circumstances to ensure that the flock remain together, and to find lost sheep at all costs. Here, too, there is not the slightest indication that the passage is being addressed solely or primarily to the leaders of the community: every Christian, to judge from the tenor of the entire chapter, has an office to fulfil

---

[7] Originally it was probably worded in the plural (see John 20:23) and reformulated in the singular by Matthew in 16:19, where Peter, Jesus' 'typical disciple', is given the authority to bind and loose. Interestingly, the rabbis also thought that their halachic decisions were vouchsafed by God and that their banishments and calendrical rules were valid before him (*Str.B.* 1, 742).

as good shepherd. Not a word is said about stern warnings and
expulsion. On the contrary, all the errant brethren are
gathered beneath the love of the Father, who does not wish to
see any of his 'little ones' go astray.[8]

It is as if the idea of the 'pure community' and the enforce-
ment of church discipline were paralyzed by the idea of the
unbounded 'great community' sheltered beneath God's love.
To put this another way, the sectarian structure of the
Matthean community is, in our discourse, counteracted by the
love of the Father. From his point of view, no one need be
relegated to the pagans and tax-gatherers. From the point of
view of Jesus' will, there are no limits to forgiveness. This
conclusion receives support from other passages in Matthew
which decisively preclude the notion of church discipline. The
Church, which is, of course, part of the 'wheat-field' and hence
of the world, has in principle both wheat and weeds. Only the
Son of Man will be able to separate the two (13:27–43); only
the king will turn the guest without wedding clothes from the
banquet hall (22:11–13). The Church is the place of those who
must prove their worth, not that of the pure. A tension-laden
impasse! The Matthean community almost certainly practised
church discipline; even 18:15–17 is, after all, Jesus' commandment! Yet it was fully aware of the limits placed, likewise by
Jesus, on a sectarian conception of the Church.

The beginning and the end of the discourse are more difficult to relate to its centre. It opens with a warning to turn back
and to become as children (18:1–5). Here readers will recall
11:25–30. A relation to the actual centre of the discourse is
brought about only in retrospect, and only implicitly: a

---

[8] The term *mikroi* ('little ones', see 18:6, 10, 14) is not easy to interpret. To judge from
11:25 it would seem to refer to all Christians. This is also the implication of 18:1–5,
where children are chosen as a model for all Christians, as are possibly the 'least of
my brothers' in 25:40 and 45. Verse 10:42, however, seemingly refers to the itinerant
missionaries, who are distinguished from the 'greater' prophets and men of righteousness. Presumably Matthew has adopted a traditional expression meaning 'ordinary' as opposed to 'special' believers (cf. 10:41–42) and employed it in a context in
which it has no matching opposite within the community and can thus serve as a
pointed term for *all* Christians.

humble sister or brother is more likely to forgive the errant. Those who can see Jesus himself in a 'little' wandering Christian (verse 5) know the infinite worth of each errant sheep. Verses 18:6–9 issue a warning not to lead the little ones astray. Presumably this is only an ancillary thought to 18:10–14: the little ones, who must under all circumstances be sought when lost, must not be led astray,[9] for they have their guardian angels in heaven with the Father.

The message is plainer in the parable of the unmerciful servant, placed by Matthew at the end of this section (18:23–35). As related by the evangelist, the parable emphasizes God's punishment of the unmerciful servant. It thereby projects the idea of God's own Judgement, which prohibits men and women from passing judgement. The gist of the parable is thus 'Judge not lest ye be judged' (7:1). Before God all men and women are *syndouloi* ('fellow servants'), which is to say, all are debtors. Before God everyone knows of the debts he or she has forgiven and not forgiven. Consequently, it is impossible for any man or woman to pass judgement. One *must* not say that a person is like a pagan or a tax-gatherer to the community[10] as this would contradict the love of the Father for his little ones and the magnanimity of the king who forgives his debtors. One may only become humble, despise no one and practise compassion. Matthew 18:23–35 is an interesting text for an 'evangelical' use of the idea of Judgement, an idea which, in this case, does nothing more than inculcate a sense of the earnestness of God's love and remove the sword of justice from mankind's very hand.

---

[9] It is difficult to say precisely what was meant by *skandalizein*. One must not explain this notion entirely on the basis of Matthew 24:10–12, as W. Thompson inclines to do in his *Matthew's Advice to a Divided Community, Mt. 17:22–18:35*, AB, 42 (Rome: Biblical Institute, 1970), 260–66, and speak of a community rent by heresies and false prophets to which the evangelist is issuing his warnings. *Skandalizein* may, as shown by 13:41, also refer to ethical sin.

[10] And yet the Matthean community said exactly that! The tension at this point cannot be resolved. Every disciplinary measure on the part of the Church implies the passing of a judgement by men and women. On the other hand, complete avoidance of church discipline would mean that the weeds and wheat in its midst could not even be distinguished by name.

RENUNCIATION OF POSSESSIONS

Luke is generally regarded as the evangelist of the poor. This is to overlook, however, that the relation to and renunciation of possessions also form a central injunction in the Gospel of Matthew.

Let me begin by surveying the relevant passages. The central section of the Sermon on the Mount, the Lord's Prayer (6:1–18), is immediately followed by section 6:19–34, which in view of its location forms a counterweight to the Antitheses. Here we find, in close succession, the passages on the treasures and the eye, Mammon, and the birds and the lilies. Their common denominator is the question of possessions. In the Mission Discourse in chapter 10 voluntary poverty is evidently a basic commandment for the disciples while underway (10:9–14), this being consistent with the poverty and homelessness of the Son of Man. Of the Parables Discourse, we should mention the traditional warning against the 'false glamour of wealth' (13:22), at the very least the only concrete ethical maxim to be found in the explanation of the fourfold parable of the field. Above all, mention should be made of the two parables of the treasure and the pearl (13:44–46), which are commonly related to divine truth, the joy of the gospel or the bliss of God's kingdom.[11] But the point of these parables lies elsewhere. The 'treasure buried in a field' and the 'merchant looking for fine pearls' (verses 44a and 45) give only the 'title' or 'topics' of the two parables, which do not begin in earnest until they recount the behaviour of the two men (*rhēma*, verses 44b-c and 46). To understand what these parables are about we must make note of where they depart from the popular parable subjects of the treasure and the pearl. The special point of our stories is that both men sell everything they have and buy the field or, respectively, the pearl. This is also what

---

[11] See the interpretations given in Luz, *Matt. II* (cf. n. 8, ch. 4), 355. Protestant exegetes in particular are fond of applying the assumptions of their own faith here, emphasizing the 'gift' of the word or of God's kingdom and completely underplaying the reaction of the human beings in the parable.

the two parables immediately recount, and what they are ultimately about.

Finally, in addition to 16:26 – 'What will a man gain by winning the whole world' (meaning all earthly wealth!) – we should above all draw attention to the story of the wealthy man (19:16–30). The last sentence of this story is then underscored by the appended parable of the talents (see 20:16).

As we have seen, the Matthean community had contact with the itinerant radicals of primitive Christianity (10:40–42), whose life and commission expressed itself in a migrant existence and missionary preaching. So strong and natural was their common bond with these itinerants that the Mission Discourse can refer to the disciples indiscriminately as itinerant and sedentary. The same point is similarly made clear in 6:19–34. The opening words of this section on possessions issue a warning against storing up earthly treasures, for every treasure binds the heart (6:19–21). To be wealthy and yet not to feel beholden to one's wealth was, for Matthew, evidently unthinkable. A man's possessions are apparently not external but central to his identity. This explains why Matthew then presents the metaphor of the 'lamp of the body' precisely at this spot (6:22–23). He wishes to stress that the way one deals with money is the determining factor in whether one is dark or light. The sharply worded passage about the inability to serve two masters underscores just how important is the question of possessions. The text that follows in 6:25–33, on the birds and the lilies, is not about inner contentment or a carefree life. The very choice of images speaks against this interpretation. If the birds do not sow and reap, if the lilies do not spin or weave, it is quite obvious with whom they are being compared: certainly not with the peasants and housewives who do just that, but with those men and women who refuse to perform this natural labour of the home and field, and for whom the heavenly Father has nevertheless provided, beyond their expectations and hopes. It is the itinerant radicals who abandon their fields and homes and set out on the road for Jesus. Our text is meant to give them encouragement. The first proverb added in verse 34 tries to impart a more general significance to the text. Verses of general validity (6:19–24, 34) thus stand side by side with words of comfort for the itinerant radicals, as in the Mission Discourse.[12] Sedentary Christians, too, can find solace in these words of comfort to the itinerant radicals. Even they who may not know at times what to eat or how to clothe themselves, they too are provided for by the heavenly Father. They, too, must direct their lives toward the righteousness appropriate to God's kingdom. Apparently the renunciation of possessions is part of that 'superior righteousness' or 'perfection' (5:48) toward which the community is heading, and of which they are to perform as much as they are able.

This view is conveyed most clearly in the story of the wealthy man (19:16–30). Jesus confronts the young man with the commandments, adding to several from the Decalogue the additional commandment of loving one's neighbour (Lev. 19:18). The young man replies that he has upheld them all. Rather than responding to this answer, Jesus then enjoins him to strive for perfection. Perfection means complete and undivided obedience.[13] It means renouncing all possessions, to be sold for the benefit of the poor, and imitating the way of Christ. The passage refers unambiguously to 6:19 and 13:44: *this* is the heavenly treasure that binds the heart to the right place.

In the history of the Church, the text we are discussing formed the starting point for the so-called 'two-level ethic', which distinguishes between those Christians who observe the ordinary commandments of the Decalogue and those who are 'perfect'. This ethic, which is deeply rooted in western monasticism, found its most significant expression in the distinction between the commandments and the so-called 'evangelical counsels'.[14] Matthew apparently thought otherwise. For him

---

[12] See p. 78 above.   [13] See p. 52 above.

[14] A classic monastic document on this way of thinking is the Syrian 'Book of Steps', the *Liber Graduum*. Matthew 19:16–21 was the *locus classicus* of an 'evangelical counsel' to an individual. The transferral of this thought to the exegesis of the Sermon on the Mount (and thus the restriction of many of its passages to the 'perfect' clergymen and monks) did not take place until relatively recently, particularly through the writings of Rupert von Deutz; see B. Stoll, *De Virtute in Virtutem*, *BGBE*, 30 (Tübingen: Mohr, 1988), 304.

there are no two levels to being a Christian. True, he is not unfamiliar with the notion of different kinds of heavenly reward – see 5:19! – but he undercuts this notion time and time again. Rather, his cognitive model is the path to perfection. Along this path an itinerant existence and the renunciation of possessions are lofty goals. Not that Matthew asks all his readers to attain this goal. His point is, however, that one must take steps in that direction, and the steps should be as large as possible.

For this reason Matthew universalizes the story in 19:23–30 and ends with a series of general instructions from Jesus. Taken by itself, wealth is dangerous and prevents men and women from entering the kingdom of God as far as is humanly possible (19:24–26). This rule applies to everyone, not simply to the young man of the story. In God's kingdom the yardstick will be reversed, and the first shall be last (19:30). This thought might initially be applied to the disciples, who have abandoned all persons and all property and become 'last' in discipleship. Matthew explains this by adding the parable of the workers in the vineyard (20:1–16), which demonstrates that the last shall be first (20:16). Whom is Matthew thinking of? In the story, of course, he is thinking of the workers who were hired last and received their wages first. But in reality? Is he thinking of the disciples who will judge the twelve tribes of Israel (19:28)? Or is he turning against those initial Christian disciples who, as the first to be called, claimed rights of precedence over the others and wished at least in heaven to rank among the great? In 20:20–21 the mother of Zebedee's two sons raises such a question. It cannot be discounted out of hand. Unfortunately Matthew did not answer it one way or the other but leaves much freedom, perhaps intentionally, to his readers' powers of interpretation.

THE SON OF MAN

Jesus' references to himself as the Son of Man appear with increasing frequency in the second half of the Gospel. There are seven such references in the main section from 12:1 to 16:20, eight from 16:21 to 20:34, seven again in the Apocalyptic

Discourse of chapters 24 and 25, and six in chapter 26. The first appears in 8:20, followed by a mere three until the end of chapter 11. 'Son of Man', then, is not a title comparable to the 'Son of God' or 'Son of David' that Matthew had painstakingly introduced in the Prologue. Indeed, the expression is not used as a title at all. Nowhere does it appear as a predicate nominative.[15] It occurs only in Jesus' own sayings, quite often as the subject. To put it more precisely, the expression 'Son of Man' circumscribes a particular manner in which Jesus speaks of himself.

In my opinion, Jesus' references to the 'Son of Man' must be seen against the background of Daniel 7 and the expectation of a heavenly judge who, according to the messianic exegesis of this text in certain Jewish circles, will appear at the end of time.[16] As regards Matthew, however, it is wrong to proceed from a fixed set of Jewish expectations for the future and to postulate that these are the 'meaning' of the expression 'Son of Man'. Rather, the Christians of the Matthean community were familiar with Jesus' references to the Son of Man. They knew that Jesus used this expression to describe his authority and his paradoxical lowliness, his suffering and resurrection, his exaltation[17] and his second coming as the Judge of the world. The expression 'Son of Man' thus refers to Jesus' path as a whole, from his earthly existence to his final consummation. At the end of this path Jesus' words take on a Danielic tinge, for

[15] The sole exception, 13:37, occurring in the catalogue of explanations of the parable of the weeds, is a special case.

[16] Among the researchers with whom I am in disagreement on this point I should like to mention T. W. Manson, *The Teaching of Jesus* (Cambridge: Cambridge University Press, 1931), 211–34; E. Schweizer, 'Der Menschensohn', *ZNW*, 50 (1959), 185–209; R. Leivestad, 'Exit the Apocalyptic Son of Man', *NT.S*, 18 (1971–72), 243–67; M. Müller, *Der Ausdruck Menschensohn in den Evangelien: Voraussetzung und Bedeutung*, *AThD*, 17 (Leiden: Brill, 1984); and V. Hampel, *Menschensohn und historischer Jesus: ein Rätselwort als Schlüssel zum messianischen Selbstverständnis Jesu* (Neukirchen-Vluyn: Neukirchener, 1990). However, since I prefer to define Matthew's understanding of 'Son of Man' from the process of communication with his Christian readers rather than deriving it from a thesis related to the history of religion, these differences of opinion are not decisive. For this reason I find myself in agreement in many respects with D. Hare, *The Son of Man Tradition* (Minneapolis: Augsburg Fortress, 1990), 113–82.

[17] Mark 14:62.

it was the conclusion Daniel had prophesied. When the readers of Matthew's Gospel heard Jesus speak of the Son of Man they heard reverberations from his other sayings with this title. In other words, the phrase 'Son of Man' evoked associations with Jesus' path in its entirety.

Now, it is noteworthy that practically all of Jesus' references in public to the 'Son of Man' occur prior to 16:20.[18] It is equally noteworthy that the majority of Jesus' sayings having to do with his present ministry are spoken in public,[19] whereas when he speaks of the impending passion and resurrection, or of the future Judgement of the Son of Man, he does so almost exclusively to the disciples, and hence for the most part after 16:21.[20] The great scene of interrogation before the Sanhedrin in 26:64 is the only place where Jesus speaks publicly of his future role as Judge of the world. By far the greatest proportion of passages treating the future fate of the Son of Man, Jesus, are therefore spoken to the disciples. This is equivalent to saying that only the disciples – that is, the community – know what sort of end Jesus will meet and who Jesus really is. The others, the Jewish leaders and the people, know none of this. They do not realize with whom they are dealing when they anathematize and persecute him. They remain in the dark.

Thus, many of Jesus' public references to the Son of Man in the first half of the Gospel serve the purpose of widening or illustrating the rift caused by the Jews' incomprehension. Christian readers, on the other hand, know more about the fate of the Son of Man and add this advance knowledge to their 'reading' of these passages. Many instances are spoken in polemical contexts: the Son of Man, unlike the foxes and the birds, has nowhere to lay his head (8:20). Christian readers know that the day will come when this same Son of Man will sit in judgement on the entire world; the scribe who wishes to follow Jesus, however, is hardly likely to be among those who

---

[18] The sole exception is 26:64.

[19] These are 8:20, 9:6, 11:19, 12:8 and 12:32. The exceptions, 13:37 and the general saying of 16:13, are found in instructions to the disciples.

[20] The exceptions are 12:40, where Jesus speaks of his resurrection publicly but in the form of a riddle, and 10:23 and 13:41, passages on the future judgement of the Son of Man that are already found here in instructions to the disciples.

board the boat with him. The Son of Man already has the authority to forgive sins (9:6), but doubt is cast on this authority by the scribes. It is he who is Lord of the sabbath (12:8), not the Pharisees, who forbid the practice of mercy on the sabbath day. It is not only John the Baptist who is mocked by this contradictory generation (11:9), but also the Son of Man, who will later rise from the dead and sit in judgement on the world. The Son of Man, like Jonah, will remain in the bowels of the earth for three days (12:40). The Pharisees who hear these words will remember them, and will have guards stationed around the grave to prevent Jesus' disciples from removing his body and feigning his resurrection, thereby causing the words of 'that impostor' to be 'fulfilled' (27:62–64). That Jesus might actually rise from the dead lay outside the realm of their imagination. Their malicious lack of understanding will then reach its culmination in the scene of interrogation before the High Council in 26:63–64. Here, for the first time in public, Jesus lifts the veil on his future and announces his elevation and second coming: 'from now on you will see the Son of Man seated at the right hand of God and coming on the clouds of heaven' (26:64). In response to this revelation the high priest tears his robes as if Jesus had committed blasphemy! Here the Judge of the world is standing before the worldly judge; the roles are reversed, and what Jesus has said metaphorically to 'this evil generation' will soon come to pass. When the unclean spirits return to the house from which they have been driven it will be worse than before (12:45).

In contrast, Jesus initiates the disciples more and more deeply into the secret of his coming path. Those who have will be given more (see 13:12). The advance Christian knowledge already available to those readers of Matthew's Gospel who identify with the disciples is deepened by Jesus' instructions. The disciples and readers are put in this position because they are with Jesus and have resolved to imitate his way. They stand on the opposite side of the 'rift' and sense something of the abyss of Israel's incomprehension and the severity of the approaching catastrophe. They are instructed by Jesus about his impending passion (17:9, 12, 22–23; 20:18–19, 28; 26:2, 24,

45). Jesus' instruction is repetitive; a good teacher always repeats what he thinks important until his students have grasped it. Jesus also teaches them that they will partake of his passion; the servant shares the fate of his master. Passion, persecution, expulsion, repudiation: these are the consequences of conformity with Christ in the life of discipleship. The community experienced these consequences at the hands of the Jews (see 10:16–23) and will encounter them again from the Gentiles (see 24:9–14). Jesus teaches them of his coming Judgement as the Son of Man, a Judgement that will also befall the community (13:41–43; 16:27–28; 19:28; 24:27, 30–31, 37, 39, 44; 25:31–46). Here, too, the good teacher repeats his message so that the disciples can learn from it. They must be made to understand what the Judgement means for them: comfort in their time of need (10:32–33; 16:27–28; 19:28) and a warning to live in compliance with Jesus' commandments. There is no guarantee that the Judgement of Jesus, the Son of Man, will exonerate them. But at least they have been prepared for it beforehand by Jesus the teacher.

For Matthew, then, the term 'Son of Man' is a cipher that embraces Jesus' path in its entirety, from his abasement to his elevation, and rekindles that path in the reader's memory. Jesus himself points out his path and helps us to understand it as a whole. Jesus' path is one of conflict and controversy with Israel. In Matthew's own day the story had reached the point of the elevation of the Son of Man. Matthew speaks quite unambiguously of the present exalted Son of Man.[21] Yet in verse 28:18 – the term 'Son of Man' does not appear, but we are told of the power given to Jesus over heaven and earth – he can also write an unmistakable allusion to Daniel 7:14. All that remains is the final stage in Jesus' path, the Day of Judgement. Matthew is preparing his readers for that day.

---

[21] In 26:64 he inserts *ap arti*.

CHAPTER 7

The final reckoning with Israel and the judgement of the community (Matthew 21:1 – 25:46)

JESUS IN JERUSALEM

With the entrance of Jesus into Jerusalem a new stage opens up in our story. Jerusalem is the city of Jesus' adversaries, the Jewish leaders (2:3–4; 15:1). It is the city in which Jesus is foreordained to die (16:21; 20:17–18). The readers know that the moment of decision is drawing near. The tension increases accordingly.

Jesus' deeds in Jerusalem cover three sequences of narrative and a discourse. The first narrative sequence makes up the exposition (21:1–27). Here Matthew relates two days of Jesus' stay in Jerusalem. First he recounts Jesus' entry into the city (21:1–11) and, from there, his appearance in the Temple (21:12–17). The focus falls on his encounter with the people. Outside the city the people prepare a triumphal reception, welcoming him as the Son of David and the Messiah (21:9; see 12:23). Entering the Temple, Jesus enacts a prophetic sign by driving out the merchants, for the house of God is to be a house of prayer. No longer does Matthew refer to a 'house of prayer for all the nations' (Mark 11:17). He knows that the time of the Temple is past, even for the nations. Most of all, however, Jesus heals the sick among the people one final time (21:14). In the Temple itself he is the healing Messiah of the poor and simple. Up to this point everything is exactly as it was: Jesus still stands in the people's favour, and they are still not far from the truth.

The second day in Jerusalem (21:18ff.) is quite different. The note is now one of judgement. Matthew relates the episode of the withered fig tree, a symbol of Israel's impending condemnation. Jesus then returns to the Temple (21:23) where he meets his opponents, the high priests and the elders of the people. The crowd, as perceived by Jesus' opponents, is present only as a foil. They ask him by what authority he is doing 'this'. In its immediate context, 'this' refers to Jesus' teachings (see 7:29). For Matthew, however, 'authority' is a mark of Jesus' ministry altogether (see 28:18). Jesus answers this question with another question: what was the authority for the baptism of John? His opponents decline to answer for tactical reasons. Again and again Matthew shows how they avoid rational argument and make a tactical escape (see 14:5; 21:46; 26:5). The question of Jesus' authority remains open. Those who abuse it out of malice do not merit an answer.

The second sequence of narrative enters without a clear break. It encompasses three parables (21:28 – 22:14). Jesus relates them to the high priests and elders arrayed against him. In effect, then, he tells three parables instead of giving a direct answer to the question of his authority. But Matthew's handling of this scene is loose. In 21:45, in place of the elders, the Pharisees appear as listeners; Jesus' opponents are interchangeable. These parables are a classic example of speaking 'in parables' to those who 'look without seeing' (13:13). The recalcitrance of Jesus' opponents does not come about as a result of these parables; they fail to understand for the simple reason *that* they are evil. In the face of such persons Jesus' parables are powerless to effect good; on the contrary, they only harden them in their evil. Thus, his opponents resolve a second time to have him arrested. Though fully aware that Jesus' parabolic discourse is directed at them, they fail to draw any consequences from it. They fail to 'understand'.

The meaning of the three parables is primarily allegorical and salvational. They inscribe a large historical arc from the biblical prophets and John the Baptist over Jesus and the community to the Day of Judgement. The short parable of the two sons (21:28–31) is told first. Originally it had a parenetical meaning emphasizing active obedience over mere affirmation of faith. Matthew gives the parable a new meaning by relating it to the coming of John the Baptist. It was not the leaders of

Israel (see 3:7) but the people (see 3:5–6) who believed in John. Matthew makes explicit use of the word 'believe', and he mentions the 'tax-gatherers' and 'prostitutes' in particular to remind his readers that the same thing had happened to Jesus. In Matthew's Gospel, John and Jesus stand side by side; they have the same message (3:2 / 4:17; 3:10 / 7:9) and suffer the same fate (11:18–19; 14:3–12; 17:10–13).

The second parable is that of the evil tenants of the vineyard (21:33–44). Here the entire biblical history of mankind's salvation – the *Heilsgeschichte* – passes review. The Deuteronomic tradition of the execution of prophets[1] is alluded to as Jesus cryptically relates how Israel mishandled and stoned the earlier and later prophets. The sending of the son is adapted to conform with Jesus' death: the son is killed outside the vineyard – Jerusalem. The scene then comes to a climax. In answer to Jesus' question his listeners, the Jewish leaders, state the punishment they themselves deserve: 'God will bring those bad men to a bad end and hand the vineyard over to other tenants, who will let him have his share of the crop when the season comes' (21:41). Jesus is thus able to make his own summing-up: 'Therefore, I tell you, the kingdom of God will be taken away from you, and given to a nation [*ethnei*] that yields the proper fruit' (21:43).[2] Is Jesus announcing the supersession of Israel by the Gentile Church in the history of mankind's salvation? Yes and no. No, because in this context he is quite clearly speaking to Israel's leaders and to no one else. No, because *ethnos* – that same Greek word for 'people' that means, in the plural, 'nations' or 'Gentiles' – cannot simply be equated with 'church'. And yet, yes, because the image of the vineyard recalls Israel, and the mention of persecuted prophets recalls its history. Yes, because the 'kingdom' was promised to the entire people. Yes, because *ethnos* is used grammatically in opposition to God's kingdom, thereby kindling expectations of an oppos-

---

[1] For further information see O. H. Steck, *Israel und das gewaltsame Geschick der Propheten*, *WMANT*, 23 (Neukirchen-Vluyn: Neukirchener, 1967).

[2] This verse is one of the classical passages used in evidence for the so-called 'theology of supersession', i.e. the notion that Israel was superseded by the Church in the history of mankind's salvation.

ing nation. Yes, because Matthew deliberately does not speak of the chosen or holy people (*laos*) but uses a term that recalls the Gentiles. Finally, yes, because Matthew's story is getting closer and closer to the final repudiation of Jesus by the entire people. But we have not reached that point yet. Thus, for the moment, the Jesus saying is initially directed to the leaders of Israel, though we can already sense more fundamental dimensions in the background.

Finally, the third parable opens our eyes to the end of history. It is the Jesuanic story, greatly revised and enlarged in the Matthean tradition, of the great feast or what Matthew now calls the wedding banquet of the king's son (22:1–14). Again messengers are sent out; again they are mishandled and killed. Here Matthew is thinking of the missionaries and prophets of his own community, who were treated no better than their biblical predecessors. Following the destruction of Jerusalem (22:7), viewed by Matthew within the terms of his own story[3] as God's punishment for Israel's repudiation of Jesus, the parable tells of the Gentile mission that is about to begin. Both good and bad alike are invited (verse 10); in this respect it reflects the parable of the weeds in the wheatfield. But the guest without wedding clothes – that is, without sufficient good deeds – is thrown out of the banquet hall into the place of darkness. Matthew ends with the Last Judgement. Here, of all things, judgement is pronounced on the Church, which will not assume the legacy of Israel automatically but only if it 'yields the fruit of the kingdom' (see 21:43).

Finally comes the third, and shortest, sequence of narrative (22:15–46). It is a series of debates. Jesus' Jewish adversaries appear once again. The opening and the concluding statements are made by the Pharisees (22:15–22, 34–40, 41–46), the major opponents of the Matthean community. Between them Jesus argues with the Sadducees. Having been reduced to silence by Jesus, they are soon aided by the Pharisees

---

[3] For Jewish interpretations of the destruction of Jerusalem as a divine punishment see Jos., *Bell*, 6:109–10 (punishment for the Zealots) and *bSchab*. 119b. The point here is that Matthew refrains from interpreting the destruction of Jerusalem eschatologically as Israel's Day of Judgement.

(22:23–32, 34). Again the people are left slightly alienated
from their leaders (verse 33). It is important to note in these
debates that Jesus emerges victorious over his adversaries.
They leave (verse 22), fall silent (verse 34) or are afraid to ask
him questions (verse 46). Here Matthew is savouring Jesus'
triumph over Judaism, a triumph withheld from his own community. According to his narrative, at least, truth has pre-
vailed. No further arguments can be levelled against Jesus,
only force and malice. That we are dealing with a Matthean
daydream, a 'triumph in spirit', becomes all too clear when we
examine Matthew's revision of the underlying Marcan source.
Compared to Mark's Gospel Jesus is even more victorious, his
opponents reduced to even greater speechlessness.

THE GREAT DISCOURSE OF WOE ON THE SCRIBES AND PHARISEES (MATTHEW 23)

We now arrive at the last great discourse in Matthew's Gospel.
Actually it consists of two discourses; Matthew has treated the
two quite unrelated discourses of chapter 23 and chapters
24–25 as a single unit in order to keep the number of discourses
down to five, a figure important to him as it recalled the five
books of the Pentateuch. Between the two parts he changes
audiences. Immediately after his proclamation of judgement
on Jerusalem (23:37–39) Jesus leaves the Temple (24:1),
prophesies its downfall (24:2) and sets out with the disciples to
the Mount of Olives. The final discourse, then, is intended for
the disciples alone, whereas chapter 23 had been delivered in
the Temple both to them and to the people. The scribes and
Pharisees, though not specifically named as listeners, are
directly addressed in the discourse no fewer than seven times.

The discourse falls into three sections. The opening section
contrasts the scribes' and Pharisees' craving for recognition
with the disciples' life of service (23:2–12). It is followed by the
seven-fold proclamation of woe on the hypocritical scribes and
Pharisees (23:13–33). Finally, there are two pronouncements
of judgement on 'this generation' and Jerusalem (23:34–39).

Taken by itself, the structure of the discourse allows us to draw two important conclusions about its interpretation. First of all, the opening section shows that its point is not merely to pronounce judgement but also to provide 'parenesis', to exhort the disciples. Admittedly it is only in the first section that the disciples are addressed directly. Here, unlike Jesus in 11:28–30, the Pharisees and scribes are shown to place heavy burdens on men and women and to crave public recognition. In this way they become antitypes of the disciples or, later, the community, where no one is permitted to boast of being a teacher or to claim the authority of a father.[4] Life in the community is to be governed by the principle of service to others (23:11). Thus, the Pharisees and scribes function as negative examples: the disciples are meant to learn from them how *not* to behave. Matthew consistently lays stress on their practice rather than their doctrines. His basic reproach is that of 'hypocrisy': their words fail to match their deeds. That the disciples must 'do everything they tell you to do' (23:2) is, of course, an example of hyperbole that, rhetorically, reaffirms the main thrust of Matthew's Gospel, the emphasis of practice over theory. In reality some of the prophecies of woe (e.g. 23:23–26) harbour different doctrinal emphases.

What applies to the opening section applies equally to the prophecies of woe that follow in 23:13–33. These, too, have a parenetical component for the community.[5] They, too, are meant to show the community how *not* to behave. Although the discourse condemns the scribes and Pharisees, the community cannot simply be assured of salvation; it stands in need of exhortation lest it suffer a similar fate.

The second important conclusion emerges from the final verses, in the two annunciations of judgement in 23:34–39. Quite imperceptibly the condemnation now spreads to the whole of Israel. It is now pronounced upon 'this generation', which has mishandled, persecuted and murdered the prophets,

---

[4] Verse 23:8 probably does not mean that rabbis (scribes) are prohibited in the community, but only that such brothers should not allow themselves to be called rabbi (*klēthēsetai*).

[5] See especially D. Garland, *The Intention of Matthew 23*, *NT.S*, 52 (Leiden: Brill, 1979), 177ff. *passim*.

sages and scribes sent to it. That the Judgement is passed on 'this generation' means that it will come soon. It is pronounced upon Jerusalem, which maligns and stones its prophets. The city itself will be destroyed. Never again will it see Jesus or his emissaries until the day of the Second Coming, and then it will be too late.[6] The end of the discourse thus nullifies the distinction between the people and its blind leaders. It is the whole of Israel that is now relegated collectively to perdition. We have already seen this done in a similar way in the Parables Discourse.

Both conclusions are fraught with difficulties. On the one hand it is refreshing to see how the Matthean community refrains from picturing itself as white sheep as opposed to the black sheep of the scribes and Pharisees. Its members know that they do not yet possess salvation but must pass muster on the Day of Judgement. On the other hand, their need for exhortation and encouragement causes them to see things in black and white. Being antitypes, the Pharisees and scribes *must* be denigrated. Whether all Pharisees or only a few really were as Matthew describes them does not interest the evangelist in the slightest. What he needs are negative stereotypes so that his community can stand out to advantage. Today we know that the Pharisees were thoroughly capable of viewing themselves with a critical eye, and that there are points of agreement between Matthew's critique and Pharisaic self-criticism.[7] Matthew's critique, however, is wholesale and therefore unjust. It reveals that there can no longer be any rapprochement between him and the Pharisees. It contains all the features associated with prejudice. Prejudice enables a person readily to find a cognitive orientation in times of difficulty.[8] Having been expelled from Pharisaic Judaism, the Matthean community needed to do just that. It had to define what it was not. But Matthew's discourse of woe is far removed from

---

[6] Verse 39 is extraordinarily difficult. I have given it the most probable interpretation here.

[7] See especially the seven classes of Pharisees in *bSot.* 22 = *Str.B.* IV 338–39.

[8] The wording is derived from U. Six, 'Vorurteile', in D. Frey and S. Greif, eds., *Sozialpsychologie: ein Handbuch in Schlüsselbegriffen* (Munich and Weinheim: Psychologie-Verlags-Union, 1987²), 366–67.

fairness or righteousness – and certainly very remote from the commandment to love one's enemy.

There is another factor that prevents Matthew from being just to the scribes and Pharisees. In the opening passages he emphasizes that their doctrine is in itself unimpeachable, and wrong only as they apply it. This makes matters decidedly too simple. In fact, Matthew measures the Pharisees not against their own doctrine but against the teachings of Jesus, in whose name and, on many occasions, with whose words he rails against them. The distinction between tithing and the 'weightier demands of the Law' (23:23), for example, is a distinction made by Jesus. The Pharisees themselves might have had a few things to say about the importance of tithing or bodily purity. But they are not given a turn to speak here, nor does Matthew allow them to speak elsewhere.

The greatest problems are posed by the shift of condemnation from the Pharisees to the entire people. In Matthew's Gospel this shift is apparent even at the narrative level. Having insisted throughout how well-disposed the people are toward Jesus, the evangelist now surprises us with an abrupt turnabout at the end of his Gospel. This turn-about is allied with the fact that Matthew's story is double-edged. Time and again he introduces experiences made by his own community with Israel. He speaks of persecution, floggings and crucifixions (23:34). Doubtless these were isolated instances which, moreover, most likely involved the Christian missionaries.[9] But for the Matthean community, now expelled from the association of synagogues in Israel, they became paradigmatic. In this way, given the community's present exclusion from Israel, the condemnation came to apply to Israel as a whole. Are we dealing with a case of frustration projected into verbal aggression?

To probe the matter more deeply we must ask about the theological origins of this aggression. The large majority of Israelites had rejected Jesus, who, to the Matthean community, represented the Messiah, the Son of God and the coming

9 See 23:34 and n. 29, ch. 1.

Judge of the world. In view of the significance Jesus had for them, Israel's repudiation *had* to be accompanied by catastrophic consequences. The harsh theology of judgement is, for Matthew and his community, a consequence of their Christology. If those who receive the disciples in reality receive Jesus, and if those who receive Jesus in turn receive God (see 10:40), then the repudiation of Jesus and his disciples can only spell disaster. Given Matthew's Christology, a harsh, dramatic, absolute and hence wholesale response to Israel's repudiation would seem to be pre-ordained from the start.

This, however, gives rise to many perplexing tensions. One line of tension arises in Matthew's narrative outline. He must present the attitude of the people toward Jesus as positive since, of course, Jesus is Israel's Messiah. Yet he must also present this attitude as negative since at that time, under the leadership of the Pharisees, Israel rejected Jesus. Another line of tension results in Matthew's portrayal of Jesus. In view of Jesus' own preaching – the gospel of the kingdom of God and the commandment to love one's enemy – Matthew should never have allowed him to speak so unfeelingly as he does in chapter 23. The message of God's love and the message of the judgement of destruction are two sides of Jesus' preaching that seem, in Matthew's Gospel, almost unreconcilable.

THE MATTHEAN ESCHATOLOGY (MATTHEW 24 AND 25)

Jesus sits down on the Mount of Olives with all his disciples. They ask him two questions (24:3): when will the Temple be destroyed, and what is the sign of his 'coming' at the end of the world? From this we can see that the destruction of the Temple and the end of the world are, for Matthew, two quite distinct things. The first is an event in history, the second the Eschaton, or end of the world. This same distinction had already been made previously in the parable of the wedding feast (22:7, 11–13). We can also see that Jesus' 'coming' and the end of the world coincide. They are both to be introduced by a single sign. In verses 29–31 Matthew takes up the 'sign of the Son of Man'. It is here that Jesus answers the second question.

At first glance Jesus' answer to the first question in 24:4–28 seems more difficult to interpret. After all, at the time Matthew wrote his Gospel the Temple had already been destroyed. The disciples' question of 'when' is therefore superfluous. How does Matthew interpret its destruction? Moreover, how does he interpret the interim period between the destruction of the Temple and the end of the world? Verses 15–22 clearly refer to the events of the Jewish War, not to events lying in some distant future.[10] Otherwise Jesus, of course, would have entirely ignored the disciples' first question. Thus, verses 15–22 represent a backward glance. They interpret the events of the Jewish War as a 'time of great distress such as has never been from the beginning of the world until now, and will never be again' (24:21). That time is now over; God has cut it short in order to save his elect (24:22). In those days there really were false messiahs and false prophets who announced the earthly return of Jesus. But the Son of Man will come from heaven, 'like lightning' (24:26–27). Following the distress of those days the end will come immediately (*eutheōs*). If we take verse 29 at its full value Matthew is living in intense expectation, for the great 'distress' (*thlipsis*) comparable to the messianic woes expected by the Jews is over.[11] The end will now follow, immediately.

This interpretation, however, makes it difficult to view the entire section of 24:4–32 as following a chronological order, and verses 4–14 as preceding verses 15–28.[12] This is obviously not the case, since 24:14 looks forward to the end of time. The end will come following the proclamation of the gospel to the Gentiles. This is exactly the perspective given in 28:19–20: the age before the end of time is the age of the Gentile mission.

---

[10] A view advanced by Gnilka, *Matt. II* (cf. n. 20, ch. 1), 322.

[11] As far as I know there is no passage that contradicts the thesis of Matthew's immediate expectation of the Second Coming. In 24:48 it is precisely the bad servant who reckons with a postponement. In 25:5 the motif of postponement, I feel, is part of the parable from the outset. Traditional passages such as 16:28, 24:33–34 or the *autē hē genea* passages virtually defy interpretation unless one presupposes an immediate expectation of the Parousia.

[12] I owe many of the insights of this section to a draft dissertation by Vicky Balabanski, Melbourne.

There is nothing in the text to suggest that verse 15 recounts the chronological continuation of the events given in verses 4–14. On the contrary, I feel that the same period of time is reported in 24:4–14 as in 24:15–28, albeit from a different perspective. Right from the outset Jesus warns against false prophets ('in my name') and false messiahs, who consider what is currently happening to be the end of time. These must be the same people as appear in verses 23–26. The wars mentioned in verses 6–8 are probably the events that occurred around the years 66 to 70 AD, now viewed from a cosmopolitan standpoint. We need only think of 68 AD, the Year of the Three Caesars, when 'nation made war upon nation, and kingdom upon kingdom'. Matthew applies to these events the apocalyptic term 'birth pangs'. In other words, they are an omen foretelling the end of time, but are not that end itself.

The verses from 9 onwards now focus on the 'inner state' of the community. It is living among the Gentiles and the object of their hatred. Verse 24:9 leads us to conclude that the Gentile mission is already underway.[13] By altering the location of Mark 13:10 (= Matt. 24:14) Matthew makes the mission directly antecedent to the end-time. Verses 11–12 once again take up the subject of false prophets. They are often thought to be identical to the false prophets of 7:15–22, those charismatic preachers who apparently neglected the practice of Jesus' commandments while working their miracles. This may well be so, but in the context of Matthew 24 one tends to think instead of the prophets of the Apocalypse.[14] One thing however is certain: with all the confusion spread by false end-time prophets the practice of love was bound to suffer in consequence.

Verses 24:29–31 describe the 'sign of the Son of Man'. Matthew uses this expression to recall 12:38–40. In that earlier

---

[13] See pp. 16–17 above and n. 24, ch. 1 (S. Brown, 'Matthean Community'). Does this mean that Matthew is championing the already extant Gentile mission of his Jewish–Gentile community? The mission cannot have been underway long, however, for 22:8–10 clearly states that it began after the destruction of Jerusalem.

[14] Cf. verses 4–5 (*planaō*) and 23–26 (*pseudoprophētai*). We cannot conclude that they are 'Antinomians' since the waning of love came about as an incidental rather than deliberate result of their preaching.

passage Jesus, asked by the Pharisees and scribes for a heavenly sign, merely responded with a riddle about the sign of Jonah, adumbrating the death and resurrection of the Son of Man. The true 'sign of the Son of Man', however, is his coming from heaven for the purpose of passing judgement.[15] It is then that the trumpets shall sound and the Son of Man shall send forth his angels to gather his chosen.[16] The nations of the earth shall beat their breasts in wild lament.

And then? What happens next? The text breaks off. Jesus turns directly to his disciples and issues a warning. The warning refers first to the near proximity of the Parousia (24:32–36), then to its surprising and catastrophic arrival (24:37–41), finally ending in verse 42 with what seems to be its definitive topic: vigilance in face of the unknown moment of the Second Coming (24:42 – 25:13). Most of these passages are parables. Though doubtless alluding figuratively to the Judgement, their main purpose is to warn. They do not depict the Judgement itself.

Such a depiction does not begin until 25:31, when the minatory interruption appears to have ended. At this point the depiction of the end-time events is resumed, followed by the Last Judgement. Verse 25:31 is a conscious reference to and resumption of 24:29–31. Though portrayed in images and allusions, the great passage on the Last Judgement in 25:31–46 is not a parable but a depiction of that Judgement. The interpretation of this passage is difficult and heatedly debated among students of Matthew. Before we take it up, however, we must first interpret the preceding section from 24:32 to 25:30, the exhortation of the community in preparation for the Judgement.

---

[15] In other words, there is no particular sign intended that will take place later. Jesus' arrival is itself the sign!

[16] The depiction refers back to 13:40–43 where, however, it is the wicked who are gathered by the angels. According to the highly generalized wording of 13:49–50 the angels separate the wicked from the good.

THE JUDGEMENT OF THE COMMUNITY

The main thrust of this exhortation clearly resides in its warning. The coming of the Son of Man is drawn with images of catastrophe: the Flood (24:38f) and the thief in the night (24:43–44). Throughout the parables the balance lies on the negative side: the evil servant and his gruesome fate (24:48–51), the foolish virgins who are left outside (25:11–12), the cautious servant who buries his master's gold (25:24–30). Twice we encounter the leitmotif, already familiar to Matthew's readers, of 'wailing and grinding of teeth' (24:51; 25:30). Our exhortation reconfirms what had already become manifest in 7:21–23, 13:36–43, 13:46–47, 18:23–35 and 22:11–14: it is the community that is being held up for judgement. The only precedence given to the community over other men and women is that it knows what it is about to confront. There is not the least certainty that it will be saved. The dominant hue in Matthew's passages on the Judgement is the fear of wailing and grinding of teeth.[17]

Matthew concludes the discourse with a depiction of the Judgement pronounced by the Son of Man on the 'sheep and goats' (25:31–46). The passage has fascinated many readers. It seems, completely unexpectedly, to make the outcome of the Judgement dependent on love of those who suffer rather than on a commitment to Jesus.[18] The people standing before the Judge of the world are surprised to learn that they have already met him beforehand on earth. Here the 'Church anonymous' seems to make an appearance. It is my feeling, however, that this fascination rests on a misreading of the text. According to 23:8 and 28:10 the brothers of Jesus, the Judge of the world, can only be Christian missionaries (cf. 18:4–6, 10), who are travelling without means of support and are thus

---

[17] Ernst, *Matt.* (cf. n. 1, Preface), 130, speaks of Matthew's 'lack of menacing undertones and overtones' and his 'avoidance of the depiction of terrifying events accompanying the end of the world'. The latter is correct, as Matthew's primary concern is exhortation. The former I find impossible to accept.

[18] Quite unlike 10:32–33.

dependent on the love and hospitality of others (cf. 10:9–14, 40–42). Our text is fully in keeping with 10:40: it is the ministering Lord, even God himself, who is present in his emissaries. The distinction between the earthly, hidden Jesus and the heavenly Son of Man corresponds, in Jesus' own sayings, to the distinction between the first-person singular 'I' and the third-person 'Son of Man' (19:28; Luke 12:8–9). In other words, Matthew feels, quite self-servingly, that the determining factor for the fate of the *ethnē* (nations or Gentiles) in the Last Judgement will be their behaviour toward the Christian missionaries. Indeed, this was previously the case with the Israel mission (10:14–15; 23:34–36).[19]

But whose fate is being determined? The meaning of *panta ta ethnē* is the second fundamental question for the interpretation of our text. To my mind it is less easy to answer than the question regarding the 'least of my brothers'. Matthew normally uses *ethnē* in reference to the Gentiles, that is, to all of humanity apart from Jews and Christians. Does this same reference apply to the more inclusive term *panta ta ethnē* ('all the Gentiles')?[20] A case for this interpretation can probably be made for 28:19. Are we dealing, then, with a judgement passed solely on non-Christians? There are two difficulties with this thesis, one literary and the other theological. Regarding the first, after the interruption at 24:31 and all the warnings given to the community in 24:32 to 25:30, one would expect the immediate pronouncement of universal Judgement (a judgement also affecting the Church) and not simply an ancillary text dealing with the judgement of non-Christians. Theologically, Matthew does not otherwise distinguish between the judgement of the community and that of the world, the wheatfield of the Son of Man (see 13:40–43, 49–50), and it would be surprising if he were to have done so here. Nor need the element of surprise necessarily imply that *ethnē* refers to non-Christians who knew nothing of Jesus. Surely the Christian missionaries they fed, clothed and sheltered did not simply remain silent about Jesus but plainly stated whom they repre-

---

[19] On this interpretation see Stanton, *Gospel* (cf. n. 9, ch. 1), 214–21.
[20] See pp. 139–40 below.

sented! To my way of thinking, the element of surprise is a literary device used to emphasize the point of the text for the benefit of the Gospel's readers. We have no cause to extrapolate from this device the existence of an 'anonymous Church'. The ambiguities probably arise from the fact that Matthew made use of a pre-existing text. The traditional text doubtless spoke of the universal Judgement pronounced upon non-Christians while the Christian men and women took their places at the side of their great brother, the Judge of the world. Matthew's community was now destined to live among and minister to the Gentiles. If asked for *his* views, he would undoubtedly have included the Christians in the Judgement to be passed on the pagan world. His principal concern was that love alone, that is, a man's works, shall determine his fate at the Last Judgement (cf. 7:21–23).[21]

In my view, then, not even this concluding passage can be said to supersede the idea of the judgement of the community, an idea that plays such an important role in 24:32 to 25:30. This raises the glaring question of the assurance of salvation. Is it possible for the deeds of Christians to undo God's love after all? Is Matthew ultimately a theological adherent of the righteousness of works, though one who uses his book to prepare his community, with all the powers at his command, for the fearful reality of the Judgement?

In an earlier section we brought our discussion of Matthew's notion of the Judgement to the temporary conclusion that everything depended on who is to be the Judge of the world.[22]

---

[21] A more difficult question is whether the Last Judgement also includes Israel. The text does not supply an answer to this question one way or the other. Up to this point the various 'judgements' passed on Israel were not eschatological in nature. This is obviously the case with the destruction of Jerusalem (22:7), which is followed by the Gentile mission. The judgement threatened upon 'this generation' in 23:36 may also refer to the destruction of Jerusalem (cf. 23:38). The 'day of judgement' includes Israel (cf. 10:15; 11:22, 24; 23:33). According to 10:15, hospitality to the itinerant radicals is the criterion applied to Israel, too. On the other hand, given that until now Matthew has almost always used *ethnē* in clear reference to 'Gentiles' (as opposed to Israel) and never to 'Israel', the readers of 24:9, 24:14 and 25:32 would not have included Israel among the *ethnē* without an explicit indication as such from the author. This interpretation will receive confirmation in 28:19 (see pp. 139–40 below).

[22] See p. 61 above.

Indeed, this seems to me to be the key to Matthew's understanding of the Judgement. Not only do the members of the community know about the Judgement and can prepare themselves for it, they also know who will be the judge. It is the Son of Man, Jesus, whom God had sent to them as Immanuel and who will accompany them on their way until the end of time. It is the Lord to whom they pray and whose way prescribes their own way. It is Jesus, not some unknown entity. Still, the knowledge that they know the Judge and that the Judge knows them, that the Judge has summoned them and accompanies them – this knowledge does not supplant the idea of judgement. Jesus is both Immanuel *and* the Son of Man; God is both Father *and* Lord. Perhaps judgement and grace belong in a dialectical relationship. A God who only loves but does not pass judgement would be a forgiveness dispenser who could be manipulated at will.[23] A God who only passes judgement but does not love, first and foremost, would be a monster.

We remain in a quandary. It seems to me that the notion of judgement according to works is a *theo*logical impossibility for the God who abides in Jesus of Nazareth and who defined himself in the resurrection. But it may be that we, as human beings, need the idea of judgement because, without it, we would be unable to take God seriously as God. The idea may be an *anthropo*logical necessity. Is this the solution to the deep dilemma underlying not only the Gospel of Matthew but the New Testament as a whole?

[23] Or, to quote Voltaire, '*Son métier, c'est pardonner*'.

CHAPTER 8

Passion and Easter (Matthew 26 – 28)

ISRAEL'S REJECTION

Chapter 26 ushers in the story of the passion, the final part and culmination of Matthew's Jesus story. Its very first verses lay the cards firmly on the table: it opens with Jesus reminding the disciples that it is now Passover, and that the time has come for the Son of Man to be crucified (26:1–2). Jesus is the first to speak; it is actually he who is in command of the situation. Only then do the high priests and elders of the nation make their appearance. They resolve, by some trickery, to have Jesus imprisoned and put to death (26:3–4). They are behindhand; they only *seem* to be the principal actors in this play. In reality they are playing 'bit parts' and will lose the game. This is what Matthew is about to narrate.

Their instrument is Judas. Matthew portrays him as avaricious and greedy (26:15). What Judas does, then, is done with evil intent. Fully knowing what he is about to commit, the traitor asks Jesus, moments before the Last Supper: 'Surely it is not I, Rabbi?' (26:25). In short, Judas is evil. But he is not the actual villain of the story. In the episode of the Blood Acre, added to the Marcan narrative from a special tradition (27:3–10), he tries to undo the evil he has perpetrated. He becomes a witness of Jesus' innocence: 'I have sinned by bringing an innocent man to his death.' But the high priests and elders turn him down: 'What is that to us? See to that yourself!' He throws his blood money into the Temple, whose destruction Jesus has prophesied. Unable to free himself of the effects of his evil deed, he kills himself. The high priests and elders use the money to purchase land for, of all things, a cemetery. It is they who are the actual villains in this play.[1]

We can see this most clearly in 26:57–68, the scene of Jesus' interrogation before the High Council. Here the high priests and elders take the leading part. Matthew paints the scene with dark hues and bitter irony. From the very outset he makes clear that the Sanhedrin is looking for *false* evidence against Jesus (26:59). The high priests base their case on perjured witnesses, just as they will later base their case on allegedly sleeping gravewatchers (28:13). The high priest 'entreats' Jesus (26:63), thereby reminding readers of Jesus' prohibition of oaths. The key verses, 63–64, seem almost to invert Peter's confession of faith in Caesarea Philippi. Once again someone proclaims that Jesus is the Christ and the Son of God. This time, however, it is not a confession, but a human word, not revealed by God. Once again Jesus answers with a reference to the Son of Man. Again he directs his glance to the future of the Son of Man. Now, in the midst of his passion, he proclaims openly that he will be elevated to the right hand of God and shall return as the Judge of the world. Thus, the divine Judge of the world stands before a worldly judge! The high priest tears his mantle, not because he is terrified at Jesus but because, so he claims, Jesus has committed blasphemy. Obviously Jesus has not blasphemed, not even by the letter of Jewish law, since he has not pronounced the name of God. The worldly judge thereupon condemns the Judge of the world and allows him to be tormented. It is a ghostly scene.

In the next scene, the interrogation before Pilate (27:11–25), the crowd is present. Pilate only seems to be the principal agent; in reality he is a supernumerary. Matthew expressly describes the release of prisoners at Passover, when the people are allowed to choose which prisoner to set free, as a Jewish custom (27:15). In so doing he ties Pilate's hands, for the

---

[1] I do not think that the homophony of 'Judas' and 'Jews' – a homophony even more striking in German ('Judas' and 'Juden') – was significant in Matthew's own time. Only in the later exegesis of the Bible did it begin to play a fateful role. For Matthew, Judas was *not* the personification of evil in mankind. If anyone played this part it was more likely the high priests and Pharisees.

governor must act in accordance with local customs. Pilate sees through the ruse of the Jewish leaders (27:18) but does nothing to hinder it. The high priests and elders, on the other hand, are the actual agents. They harangue the crowd until it clamours for the crucifixion of the Messiah, twice (27:22–23). Two further witnesses appear on behalf of Jesus' innocence, Pilate's wife (27:19) and the supernumerary Pilate himself. The latter, in accordance with biblical ritual, washes his hands (27:24).[2] He then assumes the blame that the high priests had just passed on to Judas (27:4) and hands it back to them: 'See to that *yourselves!*' The crowd does just that. In a solemn biblical formula[3] they take responsibility for the death of Jesus upon themselves and their children (27:25).[4] Matthew deliberately chooses a solemn, stark formulation for the people's self-condemnation. Deliberately he allows Jesus' prophesy of 23:35–36 to resound. At the words 'our children' he is not thinking of all the future generations of Israel over the centuries, but rather of those descendants of the crowd who will exist in the brief span of time remaining until the world ends. When he speaks of the 'entire people', employing the Greek word for 'holy people', he is, of course, not thinking in terms of historical truth. He, too, knows that there is not enough room in the tiny courtyard of the castle of Antonia or in Herod's palace to accommodate the entire population of Israel. He also knows, of course, that the whole scene is his own creation – it was lacking in his Marcan source. The truth of this gruesome scene is, for Matthew, not to be found in history. Within his own lifetime he had experienced the repudiation of Jesus by the entire people of his country, Israel. It is this experience that he has inserted into his Jesus story, explaining its meaning for that people. Matthew 27:25 is a case of staged dogmatics.

---

[2] See Deut. 21:6–9; Psalms 26:6, 73:13. Pagan rituals of absolution also existed, of course, but to the readers of Matthew's Gospel, all of whom knew their Bible, the washing of Pilate's hands was a biblical act on the part of a pagan. To them this act constituted a grotesque signal: the world is now upside down! Their attention is thus directed to verse 25 that follows.

[3] See 2 Sam. 1:16; 2 Kings 1:32f; Jer. 26:15; 51:35.

[4] In the Jewish tradition, blood guilt may apply collectively, e.g. to an entire city (see Jer. 26:15 etc.) or to the future (e.g. 1 Kings 2:32–33: 'for all time').

The terrors are nearing an end. The high priests join in the mockery of Jesus, as do a number of random bystanders and the rebels crucified with him. They mock him in the same way that evil figures in the Bible mock men of righteousness (cf. Psalm 22:7–9; Pss. Sol. 2:18). But the man of righteousness – God's Son, Jesus – chooses not to descend from the cross, remaining instead obedient to God's will (27:38–43). Thus, he 'fulfilled all righteousness' (3:15). Upon hearing these words, the Matthean community senses the double-edged meaning of this scene: Jesus *is*, of course, the Son of God, and he *will* save others – but not by descending from the cross.

The double-edged meaning becomes even more evident in the events surrounding Jesus' death. Strange things happen: darkness spreads over the entire earth, the curtain of the Temple is torn in two, the earth trembles, rocks split apart, graves open and the dead enter the Holy City (27:45, 51–53). Matthew doubtless interpreted these events as signs of the impending Judgement. Darkness is a harbinger of the Day of Judgement. Earthquakes and the bursting of rocks are part of theophany, the manifestation of God. The tearing of the Temple curtain, a sacred artefact,[5] signalizes the end of the cult. The risen dead, in anticipation of the Last Judgement, enter the Holy City where Jesus has just been put to death. Already the earliest interpreter of this passage, the glossarist of *Test. Lev.* 4:1, understood what it means: the Day of Judgement is at hand. Events now slip beyond the grasp of the high priests and the elders. God himself begins to act.

Good Friday is followed by Holy Saturday and the resurrection. Does Holy Saturday mean something to the Jewish leaders as well, or is it of significance only to the Christian community? It does indeed mean something to the Jewish leaders: it is the definitive signal of death. Matthew has, once again, staged it in masterly fashion, with scenes he presumably largely created himself. The high priests and Pharisees, in 27:62–66, recall the words with which Jesus, 'that impostor', explained the sign of Jonah (12:40). Unbelieving and sus-

---

[5] See *syr.Bar.* 6:7–10.

picious, yet cautious, they hope to prevent the disciples from staging a resurrection 'after three days' and thereby creating a new deception worse than the first.[6] They install guards and secure the grave, as they understand such things (cf. verse 65!). These gravewatchers become witnesses of Easter, but in such a way that at the sight of the angel on the morning of the resurrection they are struck 'as if dead' from shock (28:4).[7] God has spoken; for Matthew, the awakening of Jesus is not a question of subjective faith but a clear act of God impinging on the physical world. The only defence the high priests and elders can muster is fraud (28:11–15). Again they offer money, this time to the gravewatchers; money accompanies their evil throughout the story of the passion. They ensnare themselves in an obvious lie from which they can only extricate themselves by using their good connections with the governor, Pilate. They base their case on the gravewatchers as their principal witnesses, whose 'evidence' consists in a claim that they were asleep at the crucial moment. In this way the rumour of the stealing of Jesus' body has remained in circulation among Jews 'to this day' (28:15).

Thus ends one of the two narrative threads in Matthew's story of the passion and Easter, namely the story of the conflict between Jesus and the Jewish leaders. The conflict comes to a close with the evangelist's first outlook into his own present day. What does that outlook signify? It signifies a devastating verdict on the Jewish leader's claims to be the leaders of Israel. Does it signify the end of the election of the chosen people of Israel, who are now left behind in untruth? This would seem to be the inference of 21:43, 23:34–39 and, especially, 27:25. This same inference is suggested by the fact that Matthew now uses, for the first time, the word 'Jews'. Previously, following Palestinian custom, he only employed this term when the Gentiles spoke of Israel (2:2; 27:11, 29, 37). On the other hand, it is

---

[6] An allusion to 12:45.

[7] In the Gospel of Peter, at a later historical stage in the transmission of this material, the gravewatchers become the actual eye-witnesses of Easter, thereby transforming the Resurrection into an objective and describable event (*Ev.Petr.* 8–11). See E. Hennecke and W. Schneemelcher, *Neutestamentliche Apokryphen in deutscher Übersetzung*, 1 (Tübingen: Mohr, 1987⁵), 186–87.

noteworthy that Matthew avoids the definite article in verse 15 and speaks merely of 'Jews'. Is he intimating that not all Jews believed the rumour of the stealing of Jesus' body?

THE DISCIPLES' PATH TO THE GENTILES

The story of the passion is also significant for an understanding of discipleship. It is precisely in this scene that Jesus serves as a model and exemplar. The story of Gethsemane in 26:36–46 is especially important in this respect. Jesus arrives 'with them'[8] at Gethsemane in order to hold vigil and pray at their side. Jesus prays with the words of the Lord's Prayer: 'My Father . . . Thy will be done' (26:39, 42). He will be obedient to the will of the Father and allow himself to be arrested without trying to resist evil. The disciples are told to hold vigil. 'Holding vigil' is, according to 24:42 and 25:13, a symbol of Christian life; prayer symbolizes obedience to the will of the Father.

The disciples are unable to do either. They fall asleep. Throughout the story of the passion Matthew's description of them is ambivalent. They vacillate between obedience and disobedience. They are allowed to partake of the Lord's Supper and the remission of sins that takes place on that occasion (26:28). They swear loyalty to Jesus (26:33, 35). But at the dramatic seizure of Jesus they flee. Peter becomes a negative example of how disciples should not behave: he refuses to confess his faith in Jesus before other men (cf. 10:32–33), but immediately regrets his cowardice and sheds bitter tears (26:75).[9] To the very end of the story Matthew maintains his ambivalent picture of the disciples. They do not vanish as completely as in Mark's Gospel; in 28:8 the women know as a matter of course where they are to be found. Even the women, who remain present until Jesus' crucifixion, 'watching from a distance' (27:55), partake of the ambivalent

---

[8] See p. 31 above.

[9] Peter's denial of Jesus (26:69–75) is followed almost immediately by the story of the death of Judas (27:3–10). The latter, too, regrets his deed – but it is too late to do him any good! Peter's repentance, however, abrogates Jesus' hard declaration in 10:33. There is no coherent explanation for this contradiction on the synchronous textual level.

portrayal of the disciples: their mixture of fear and joy at the grave (28:8–10) corresponds with the disciples' mixture of adoration and doubt during their encounter with Jesus on the Galilean mountain (28:16–17). For Matthew, the ambivalence of the disciples' behaviour – the intermingling of faith and doubt, of obedience and failure – apparently constitutes the reality of discipleship. The disciples' experiences, for Matthew, mirror the real experiences of Christian men and women.

The decisive text about the disciples is, however, the final passage in the Gospel, the appearance of Jesus on the mountain before the Eleven in 28:16–20. It is my belief that this passage – apart from the triadic baptismal formula in verse 19, which was probably traditional in the community – is entirely redactional. Every word of it counts; it abounds in associations with earlier passages. In verse 18 Jesus reveals himself on the mountain to be he whom God has granted all powers of heaven and earth. There is an allusion to Daniel 7:14, a passage familiar to the community. At the opening of the Gospel, likewise on a mountain, Jesus rejected the devil's offer of world domination. Now the circle has come full close; the path of the obedient Son of God has reached its destination.

The Lord of the world sends forth his disciples to turn all men and women into disciples (verse 19a). In Matthew, 'discipleship' is a paraphrase for the Christian life. There is no other way to be a Christian than to learn continually from Jesus, to obey him, and to gather experiences in his presence. Who is called to discipleship? Again, the translation of *panta ta ethnē* ('all the nations/Gentiles') is subject to debate.[10] In the biblical tradition, as well as in Matthew's Gospel, *ethnē* generally means 'Gentiles'. However, the boundary to 'nations' is not hard and fast. In the passage we are discussing, there are two considerations that argue in favour of the translation 'all the Gentiles'. First, in the immediate context, a contrast arises with the conspicuous 'Jews' in verse 15. In a larger context, there is a clear allusion to 10:5–6, where Jesus forbade the disciples to go to the Gentiles.[11] It is this very instruction which

[10] See pp. 130–31 above.
[11] The catchwords in common are *ethnē* and *poreuesthai*.

the risen Jesus now reverses. Moreover, we must also consider the sharp contrast between Israel and the Gentiles. This contrast, already visible in the Prologue (especially in chapter 2), is present in later passages as well.[12] The Gospel's readers have been prepared for a volte-face. I feel that the Great Commission must be understood as just such a volte-face: from now on the disciples are to turn to the Gentiles.[13] On the surface of the story, 'now' means Easter. But to Matthew's original readers 'now' referred to their own day, a time when the Gentile mission was apparently still a new or controversial task for the community. Having failed in Israel, the community has been assigned a new task by its Lord.[14]

Mission means 'teaching', passing on what the sole teacher, Jesus, did for his disciples. The substance of the mission is Jesus' commandments. The words 'everything I have commanded of you' is a phrase taken from the Bible (Exodus 29:35). The 'gospel of the commandments' is rooted deep in biblical thought, not only linguistically but also in its very essence.[15] 'Everything' is in keeping with the notion of perfection. In other words, the community is meant to distinguish itself from the rest of the world by its works (cf. 5:16). But Matthew goes beyond the commandments and concludes his Gospel with the promise of Jesus' continued presence. Jesus is the Immanuel, the 'God with us'; his assistance, his power, his commandments and his teachings are a constant foundation of life.

In short, Matthew concludes his Gospel in a manner quite unusual for Protestant sensibilities, by intermingling grace and commandments, the 'indicative' and the 'imperative' of sal-

---

12 Matthew 8:5–13; 10:5–6; 15:21–28.
13 In consequence, 24:14 should presumably be interpreted in the same way, even though it does not contain any clear signals.
14 The passage doubtless does not imply that all missionary work among Jews is henceforth prohibited. It more probably means that the community should no longer view its life-work as consisting in the Israel mission.
15 It is tempting to think that Matthew, in 28:16–20, adopted wordings from the final text of the Hebrew Bible, 2 Chr. 36:23. Would this make a new Bible of Matthew's Gospel, which begins with the catchword *genesis* and frequently incorporates biblical motifs, particularly from the Book of Exodus? Some thoughts on this point can be found on p. 32 above. Nevertheless, the relation with 2 Chr. 36:23 is unspecific and highly superficial.

vation. Jesus' commandments are the gospel that his disciples owe to the world. They represent the Father's will to redeem his world. But they are not the will of a distant and unreachable God. On the contrary, the 'God with us' will remain with his community always, to the end of time, helping it, teaching it, and standing by its side as it faces new challenges.

CHAPTER 9

Concluding thoughts

MATTHEW AND JESUS

For Matthew, to be a Christian is to be a pupil of Jesus. Jesus and his commandments are the standard by which he wishes to be measured. But does Matthew himself live up to this standard? For Matthew, 'Jesus' is what he found handed down in his sources, especially Mark and Q. Today we know both more and less about Jesus than he did. We know more because we have gone some way towards distinguishing between Jesus and his post-Easter interpreters. We know that Jesus and the post-Easter Lord who spoke through his prophets are not simply identical. Yet we know less because the corpus of genuine Jesus material has shrunk. We also know less because our discretionary leeway for deciding what is or is not authentic to Jesus is very large.[1] At all events, by asking about the relation between Matthew and Jesus we are applying a modern question to our Gospel – a question which, however, is not alien to its original intention. On this matter I would like to offer the following points for consideration.

(1) For Matthew, 'Jesus' meant the living Jesus who accompanies his community on its way in the present. When Matthew equated the gospel Jesus intended for the Gentiles with his commandments (rather than, say, with the voice of the Spirit!), he did not simply mean a Jesus who was dead and

---

[1] Just how far away we are from consensus can be seen by comparing the books on Jesus by E. P. Sanders, *Jesus and Judaism* (London: SCM, 1985), T. Holtz, *Jesus aus Nazareth* (Berlin: Union, 1979) and J. Crossan, *The Historical Jesus: the Life of a Mediterranean Jewish Peasant* (San Francisco: Harper, 1991).

immutable. On the contrary, Jesus was such a living presence that he was able to retract and reverse his earlier commandment to minister to Israel only. Matthew was able to adapt Jesus' sayings to contemporary circumstances, or even to write them afresh. This was, for him, another aspect of the living quality of the risen Jesus. Yet it was in itself nothing extraordinary for a Jew: the Torah, too, was adapted again and again to contemporary circumstances, and even at times written afresh. Not only did Matthew recast the Marcan story of Jesus, he wrote it anew, especially at the beginning and end of his book, in order to make it the fundamental story of his community and to bring it into line with their experiences. For Matthew, the story of the historical Jesus had to reflect, at one and the same time, the story of the risen Lord with his community. This, too, is nothing unusual for a Jew, who knows that the fundamental story of God with his people must constantly be retold. For Matthew, then, Jesus is both the living and the resurrected Lord. For this reason alone he is not simply to be measured against our knowledge of the earthly Jesus. On the other hand it is clear that Matthew did not want to create a new Jesus. To an astonishing degree he held fast to his traditions; his rendering of the sources was virtually complete and intact. Matthew's story of Jesus and his interpretation of Jesus' preaching were not allowed to be arbitrarily remote from Jesus himself.

(2) Jesus saw himself as an ambassador of God's future kingdom, part of which was simultaneously embodied in his own presence. In Matthew these two factors seem to fall asunder. Jesus, and thus the beginning of the story, already lie in the past; his past history can be told. The kingdom of God, however, lies in the future; only later will it be possible to enter it. Similarly, the experience of salvation is more closely bound to the past, while the Judgement is bound to the future of God's kingdom. But these departures from Jesus' thought should not be over-emphasized. Matthew felt that Jesus' past, far from being over and done with, determines the present. Matthew's present abounds in experiences with Jesus; no unsanctified intervening period has arisen. On the other hand, the future of

God's kingdom is nigh. In other words, Matthew does not view his own day as an interim period, as a special epoch distinct both from Jesus and end-time. In this respect he differs greatly from Luke, and is thus closer to Jesus than the third evangelist.

(3) Matthew stresses programmatically that Jesus has 'fulfilled' the Law and the prophets. This programme, as we have seen, goes some way toward answering the demands of his contemporary predicament. That Jesus is the true inheritor of the Law and the prophets was contested by most Israelites, and Matthew, a representative of the true Israel summoned by Jesus but expelled from the association of synagogues, had to supply a fundamental answer on this point. How does he stand here in relation to Jesus? Since time immemorial commentators have debated to what extent Jesus himself abided by the Law. According to our interpretation today, Mark and Matthew, to name only two, represent opposing sides on this issue. But Matthew's redactional rewriting of Mark 7:1–23 in 15:1–20 reveals that he saw no more opposition to Mark here than between 5:17 and the 'primary' Antitheses. Matthew thinks in terms, not of opposition, but of complementarity. He appears not to have censored his Jesus sources. On the contrary, he 'channelled' them through his own interpretation, safeguarding the Antitheses from an antinomistic misunderstanding and protecting Mark 7:15–23 from the notion that Jesus fundamentally annulled the law of purity.

But how should we answer this question today? Jesus' relation to biblical Law is one of those questions that scholars have been unable to clarify completely. Thus, all I can do is put forward an opinion based on my own image of Jesus. To my way of thinking, Matthew, by saying that Jesus fulfilled the Law and the prophets, may have narrowed Jesus down to a basic principle but cannot be said to have falsified him. And that, unfortunately, is where we must let matters rest.

(4) The question most difficult to answer is whether Matthew, with his theology of Israel, came into fundamental conflict with Jesus' teachings. Indeed, this conclusion seems unavoidable: Jesus knew that he was sent to God's people, Israel, and not, as Matthew 10:5–6 rightly maintains, to the

Gentiles. True, he viewed the concept of the Israelite nation broadly, from the standpoint of a person living on its periphery. But he did not transcend the idea of nationhood. The step leading from Jesus to the thought that the kingdom will be taken away from Israel is a very long one. To put it more strongly, this notion turns Jesus' teachings upside down. God's love, as preached by Jesus, must not be delimited by man, and most certainly not to the exclusion of the people of Israel. The commandment to love one's enemy – the commandment that corresponds to God's love – seems in texts such as Matthew 23 to have vanished completely.

None the less, it is precisely in such anti-Jewish texts that we find a genuine Jesuanic line of tradition upon which Matthew was able to draw. Jesus himself prophesied the near proximity of the Last Judgement. The announcement of the Judgement is a central part of his preaching.[2] At the same time Jesus attached crucial importance to himself in this Judgement: anyone who acknowledges him before men will be acknowledged in turn by the Judge of the world when he arrives with the angels of heaven (Luke 12:8). It does not matter whether the earthly Jesus did or did not identify in one way or another with the coming Son of Man and Judge of the world; even without such an identification the claims that Jesus raises for himself boggle the mind. Only the house of those 'who hear these words of mine and act on them' (7:24–27) will stand! Jewish teachers spoke in such terms only of the Torah, never of themselves. If Matthew takes this aspect of Jesus at its full value and has to note that Israel, in his own day, failed to acknowledge Jesus, it is only a small step to the theology of Israel's condemnation that he espouses. Moreover, he can also draw on a by no means small number of logia on the Judgement, many of them genuine. With Jesus, these words probably had the character of an urgent admonition to penitence; with Matthew, they take on an aspect of inescapable condem-

---

[2] Further comments on this frequently 'overlooked' aspect of Jesus' preaching can be found in M. Reiser, *Die Gerichtspredigt Jesu*, *NTA.NF*, 23 (Münster: Aschendorf, 1990).

nation.[3] The anti-Jewish theology of the judgement of Israel is thus not simply an attempt on the part of the evangelist to overcome the pain of separation from Israel; it is also clearly rooted in Jesus' own teachings. If Matthew deepens these roots he is not simply being a disloyal pupil of Jesus. We may not like to hear this; the announcement of the Judgement is among the least popular and most frequently suppressed aspects of Jesus' preaching. Matthew recalls it to mind, and at the same time confronts us with the question of whether that which he has sundered – God's love for Israel and God's judgement on Israel – can really have been conceived as a unity in Jesus' own thought.

MATTHEW AND PAUL

Paul, the New Testament advocate *par excellence* of a theology of pure grace? Matthew, the New Testament advocate *par excellence* of a theology of deeds, perhaps even of a righteousness of works? Do Matthew and Paul stand at opposite poles in the New Testament?[4] The answer must be: yes, superficially. And yet this superficial impression seems to find a certain confirmation in the history of their subsequent reception and impact. Matthew's is the Gospel *par excellence* not only of the Church but specifically of monastics, the mendicant friars of the Middle Ages and the marginal movements of the Reformation, especially the Anabaptists. Paul is the classical Church Father of the major Protestant denominations, whose principal gospel was never Matthew but John.[5] Of course this formulation is highly simplified; but it is nevertheless correct in all essentials.

Historically, Matthew and Paul seem to have no points of contact with each other. Pre-Matthean texts such as 5:18–19, dealing with the upholding of even the lesser commandments of the Law, or 10:5–6, prohibiting the mission to the Gentiles

---

[3] See, for example, Matt 8:11–23 (logion of Jesus); 11:20–24 (provenance highly uncertain); 23:34–6, 37–9 (words of the risen Lord).

[4] See R. Mohrlang, *Matthew and Paul: a Comparison of Ethical Perspectives*, *MSSNTS*, 48 (Cambridge: Cambridge University Press, 1984). This important monograph on the subject tends to minimize the tensions between the two.

[5] See M. Luther, 'Vorreden zum Neuen Testament', *WA.DB*, 6.

and Samaritans, illustrate the distance between the two men. Nowhere does Matthew's Gospel suggest that its author may have been familiar with Paul or his epistles. Nor is there any trace of a polemical debate with Paul, that arch-enemy of so many later Jewish–Christians. If Matthew's Gospel originated in Antioch, the lack of contact is striking. But Antioch was a large metropolis which did not even have a central synagogue, much less a central point of assembly for Christians. It is highly conceivable that there were many house churches in Antioch with little contact between them. Seen against this background, Ignatius' persistent demands for unity with the bishop take on a more distinct colouration.

If we take Matthew's demand to uphold the Law at its full value,[6] his distance from Paul becomes great indeed. In Paul's own day – that is, in the generation preceding Matthew – the Galatian 'Judaists', who combined an active Gentile mission with a demand for at least partial conformity with the Law, were probably more closely related to Matthew than was the non-law-abiding Gentile missionary Paul. The notion that the Law is a yoke which no one has yet been able to bear, and which in no case should be placed on the shoulders of the Gentiles (Acts 15:10–11), is completely alien to Matthew. On the contrary, Jesus' commandments, which fulfilled rather than abolished biblical Law, are the quintessence of his Gospel. Within the New Testament canon the Letter of James is, to a certain extent, related to Matthew. But its author had already taken the decisive step away from the ritual law that distinguishes Jews from Gentiles: the *only* thing that counts, for him, is the 'perfect law that makes us free' (James 1:25), that is, the moral law. Although the moral law is also of *primary* importance to Matthew, the one is not meant to exclude the other (see 23:23). We know what the author of James thought of Paul, to whom he bears closer affinities than to Matthew (see James 2:14–26). Matthew, in turn, is even further removed from Paul

---

[6] Extrapolating from Matthew 5:17–19, I assume that ceremonial law also remained binding on the Matthean community; see pp. 14 and 57–58 above. An opposing view can be found in Strecker, *Weg* (cf. n. 18, ch. 1), 143–47, who maintains that Matthew rejected ceremonial law.

than James. This leads me to think that Matthew and Paul, had they known one another, would certainly not have struck up a strong friendship.

The two men have radically different relations to Judaism. For Paul, 'Judaism in practice' (Gal. 1:13–14) is a principle in sharp opposition to Christian faith. It is constituted by abiding within the Law, which is governed in turn by the principle of works: he shall live who does what the Law requires (Lev. 18:5; cf. Gal. 3:10–12; Rom. 10:5). This 'works principle' is counterposed to the righteousness that comes by faith: he shall live who receives as a gift this righteousness, which is always nearby (Rom. 10:5–8). Christ freed mankind from the principle of works. Accordingly, Paul sees a break in the path leading from Judaism to Christianity: what used to be precious to him he now considers 'dung' (Phil. 3:7–9). This is fully in keeping with his experience on the road to Damascus, where a single stroke brought about a radical conversion and turn-about in his life. Thus, for Paul, Judaism and Christianity are two fundamentally opposing principles.[7] In the course of his theological evolution he had to rethink anew what it means that the God of Jesus Christ was also the God of Israel – more than that, the giver of the Law which is holy, just and good (see Rom. 7:12!). Pauline theology, one might say, has to struggle with Antinomism from its very beginning.[8]

Matthew thinks quite differently. He sees no rupture between Judaism and Christianity. On the contrary, the Jesus who fulfilled the Law and the prophets represents the true Israel. He sees the controversy with other Jewish groups, especially that with the Pharisees, primarily as a dispute over what constitutes the true Israel. In its own self-understanding the Matthean community was a Jewish group that claimed to represent the true Israel. By no means did it see itself, as did the Pauline Church, as a *new* entity distinct from Israel, namely as

[7] See esp. E. P. Sanders, *Paul, the Law and the Jewish People* (Philadelphia: Fortress, 1983), 17–64.

[8] The editor, Professor J. Dunn, would accentuate this quite differently; see his *The Theology of Paul's Letter to the Galatians* (Cambridge: Cambridge University Press, 1993) in the same series.

the Body of Christ embracing Jews and Gentiles alike. Consequently, for Matthew, there is no rift between Jewish and Christian faith, between the Bible and Christ, or between the Law and the Gospel. There is only a rift between him and those leaders of Israel and their followers who do not do as Jesus teaches, and who (a typically Jewish train of thought) exclude themselves from God by virtue of their deeds.

The profound difference between the two men becomes symbolically clear in their understanding of righteousness. Paul appropriates 'righteousness' as a Christological term. What 'God's righteousness' consists in becomes manifest when men and women experience the way God acts upon them through Christ. To say that God reveals his own righteousness in Christ is to say that he defines himself through Christ. For Matthew, conversely, 'righteousness' is that which God in his love demands of men and women. 'Righteousness' means the human path which Jesus' disciples must travel when they allow themselves to be taught, led and accompanied by the Immanuel.[9]

In sum, I sense a profound tension between Matthew and Paul, perhaps even an abyss. They proceed from the same Jesus Christ, but interpret him in very different ways.

Where does this tension come from? Of course, the traditions that conditioned both men were quite different. In Matthew's case it is the Jesus tradition: it is Jesus, his story and his teachings that determine faith. In Paul's case, it was faith in Jesus' expiatory death and resurrection that formed the basis of his own theological reflections. Most of all, the personal experiences of the two men were quite different. We know Paul well. It is my belief that his theology cannot be understood apart from his biography. His shattering experience before the gates of Damascus left its mark on his entire theology. Christ was, for Paul, something radically new that called to question his previous life as a Jew. Precisely because his theology derives from such a personal experience it is a highly *individual* theology. Again and again Paul elaborates in his theology the way

[9] See p. 33 above.

in which he *became* a Christian. Our knowledge of Matthew, on the other hand, is indirect and far less complete. I believe that his Gospel was undergirded not so much by personal experiences as by the experiences of his community. Never did he suffer a rupture with his Jewish faith. Matthew was motivated by the animosity of, and conflict with, other Jews who wanted nothing to do with Jesus. He was also motivated by the experiences of his community: the gradual weakening of its faith, its want of courage in prayer, its backwardness on the path of righteousness. His constant concern is the question of how to *remain* a Christian. In far greater measure than Paul, Matthew is a theologian of the *community*. For both men, however, their theology was not a matter of individual 'choice'. It is an expression of their lives, their experiences, their biography and their situation. In this sense, then, their theology is contextual. Hence, even for us later readers of Matthew or Paul, there is no way to make a general decision regarding the truth of the one or the other. We can only make a decision conditioned by our situations, biographies and personal experiences. Accordingly, the choice of 'Matthew or Paul' can never be discussed in the abstract, divorced from one's own experiences.

For all their many differences, there are also deep points of convergence between the two men. These points are all the more conspicuous for being expressed, generally, in quite different language. I can only sketch several of them here.

(1) Matthew does not advocate a theology of the righteousness of works either. I need only recall a few important observations regarding his Gospel: the precedence given to the story of Jesus over his commandments; the idea of 'Immanuel' that frames his entire Gospel; Jesus' presence in his community, as revealed, for example, in the miracles; the element of surprise in the Last Judgement, rendering impossible any rewards for calculated action.[10] Finally I recall Matthew's theology of prayer. The centrepiece of the Sermon on the Mount is the Lord's Prayer; the heart of all human daring is the trusting cry of the weak and frail to the *kyrios*.[11] Matthew knew full well

[10] See pp. 31–34, 47, 60 and 66–69 above.
[11] See pp. 49–51, 67 and 94–95 above.

about the breadth of grace, for he had before his eyes the constant weakness and failure of human beings, Christian and otherwise. Not only Paul but Matthew too understood the priority of grace, although, now that that grace had been preached in his community for half a century, he strengthened the obligations which grace imposes. The primacy of grace in the theology of Matthew's Gospel is also evident in its ecclesiological structures: the idea of the path of righteousness prevents the community from falling apart into 'beginners' and 'advanced learners'.[12] There is no one in the Matthean community who is greater than 'these little ones'.

(2) Paul, too, advocates a theology of deeds. This is not the place to explain my point in detail, but I can at least submit that Pauline faith is always operative in love (Gal. 5:6). I would like to recall that the justification of men and women takes place *in* and not prior to their deeds, though it otherwise makes sense that Paul regards the intermixture of indicative and imperative as a paradox (cf. Rom. 6:12–23). I would also like to recall that Paul, too, considered judgement on the basis of works to be a constitutive part of theology and not merely a left-over remnant of Jewish thought. I do not feel that the strict separation of individuals from their deeds – an idea of cardinal importance to Reformation theology – is truly congruent with Paul's thought. Nor do I feel that, for Paul, sin is something 'transempirical', as though relevant only to a relationship with God and not to deeds that effect others. Thus, to my way of thinking, Paul and Matthew do not stand opposed on this point. Indeed, Matthew can serve again and again as a corrective for any attempt to underplay ethics in favour of faith, and the outer life in favour of the inner life, by appealing to Paul.

(3) Matthew, too, realizes why men and women cannot constitute their personal being through works. I am thinking especially of Matthew 6:1–18, that significant passage on God, who sees what is done in secret and thwarts all our attempts to show ourselves as other than we really are. It is important that the Antitheses, which are entirely directed to external deeds,

---

[12] See pp. 55–56, 78–79 and 110 above.

are thus supplemented by a text dealing with the internal dimension of righteousness. It is equally important that the kernel of 'superior righteousness' is prayer. For Matthew, too, a relationship to God is constitutive for personal being. The exterior and interior dimensions of righteousness, love of mankind and love of God, action and prayer: all of these coalesce in Matthew just as love and faith coalesce in Paul.

(4) The Matthean principle of fulfilment of the Law, and the Pauline principle of freedom from the Law, are mutually exclusive. This is not the place to explain why Matthew treats the Law as a helpful directive and an 'easy yoke', whereas Paul sees it functioning as a distraction leading men and women to bondage and sin. It is here in particular, I feel, that the peculiar route of Paul, a former 'zealot' for the Law and a persecutor of Christians, plays a part. Here, in sharp contrast to Paul, Matthew is able to make us aware that God's command may be something merciful and helpful: it lays a claim on men and women, thereby imparting significance to their lives; it signifies a helpful protest against the rule of money (6:24!), violence (5:38–48) or power (20:25–28). Yet Matthew and Paul reveal much in common when, directly or indirectly, they construe the Law as an ordering principle for Christian life. Both share a belief that Christ is the *norma normans* of the Law. Both believe that the heart and core of the Law is love (22:34–40; Rom. 13:8–10). Both believe that listening to men and women takes precedence over the imposition of religious principles (compare, for example, 12:1–18 and 1 Cor. 8:6–13).

(5) Another point of contact between Matthew and Paul is the universality of faith in Christ. Christ is granted *all* power in heaven and on earth; he is Lord of *all* men and women and *all* nations. Matthew represents a Jewish–Christian community that has burst the bonds of its own particularism. Paul is more thorough-going in this respect in that he refrains from forcing Jewishness upon Gentiles as the precondition for the bond with Christ. On this point Matthew, as far as we can see, was pre-Pauline. Yet we must not forget that Jesus, too, was pre-Pauline on this same point; Paul represents an important step beyond him. Both, however, moved in the same direction.

Between Matthew and Paul, then, there is a fruitful and productive field of tension. They are not antipodal. Neither are they simply brothers. They can complement one another by pointing up, with their strengths, the other's weaknesses. But most of all, the differences between them, together with all the other various attempts to draft the New Testament, can prevent us from succumbing to mindless Biblicism and can compel us, as today's receivers of their thought, to take responsibility for our faith *ourselves* in dialogue with them.

MATTHEW AND CHURCH HISTORY

The Gospel of Matthew very soon became the most popular and most important gospel of the Church. It was quickly disseminated throughout the larger body of the Church: even the author of the First Letter of Peter may have presupposed an acquaintance with it. Surely Matthew's was 'the Gospel' to the author of the *Didachē*; it was obviously well-known in his community, and he himself proceeded from it, though he did not quote from it directly. Similarly Ignatius, the Bishop of Antioch, was most likely familiar with Matthew's Gospel, even if he was probably not very fond of it. With regard to other writings of the early second century, such as the two letters of Clement or that of Barnabas, the points of contact with Matthew are less certain.[13]

The rapid dissemination of the Gospel of Matthew is astonishing. Part of the reason for this was, of course, that the early second-century Church was strongly orientated on traditions, and that communities exchanged Gospels no less readily than Pauline letters. But the Gospel's dissemination would not have been possible if the Jewish–Christian Matthean community had not reached out toward the Great Church and agreed to undertake the Gentile mission, thereby becoming integrated in the larger body of the Church. Thus, the Gospel of Matthew suffered a fate completely different from that of the Jewish–

---

[13] See W. D. Köhler, *Die Rezeption des Matthäusevangeliums in der Zeit vor Irenäus*, *WUNT*, II/24 (Tübingen: Mohr-Siebeck, 1987).

Christian Nazarene and Ebionite Gospels written just a short while later.

From the middle of the second century Matthew's Gospel clearly became the most important Gospel of the Church. One reason for this was undoubtedly that unlike Mark and Luke, it was held to be the work of an apostle. Another important reason, probably, was that unlike Mark it contained a very large number of Jesus' sayings. In the second century, we should recall, 'the Lord', not the Scriptural canon, formed the underlying authority of the Church, and the 'recollections of the apostles' (Justin, *Apol.* 1,66,3) provided the fundamental tradition upon which the words of the living Lord Jesus were recast for the present. At that time Jesus' sayings were far more important than the single stories about his life. This explains why Matthew's Gospel was accorded greater significance than Mark's. But without a doubt the effect of his Gospel resided in the individual sayings collected within it rather than in its overall narrative outline – its 'Jesus story' – though the latter was obviously a matter of utmost concern to the evangelist himself. Hardly any notice was taken of the narrative of Matthew's Gospel in its subsequent reception by the Church. Finally, Matthew's Gospel may well have commended itself by its five discourses, which arranged the words of Jesus in an attractive and catechistically useful order. Papias' remarks on the Gospel of Mark show that considerations of this sort were indeed taken seriously in later Church circles.[14]

A history of the impact of Matthew's Gospel throughout the centuries would go beyond the limits of this slender volume. The important point to note, however, is that before the days of the Enlightenment the Gospels were always perceived as witnesses of Jesus, not as special books in their own right. Thus it happened that Matthew's Gospel became the major vessel of the Jesus tradition; there were many more commentaries written on it than on Luke – and vastly many more than on Mark – for the simple reason that it provided the most important access to Jesus. Equally significant is the fact that what

---

[14] Euseb., *H.E.* 3, 39, 14–15.

was received and handed down from Matthew were generally isolated passages or pericopes rather than larger sections. Not only does this reflect the time-honoured opinion that the Gospels are important for being 'recollections' of the Lord, it also mirrors the day-to-day reality of the Church: isolated pericopes were important for lections during the service, for homilies and for instruction. The fundamental differences between the Gospels were largely overlooked until the days of the Humanists and Reformers, and above all the adherents of the Enlightenment, who began to read the four Gospels as historical documents. Those matters that have occupied our attention in this little volume – namely Matthew's distinctive narrative outline and his redactional work on Mark and the Sayings Source – did not fully come into their own until the second half of our own century. Redaction criticism and narrative criticism are offsprings of the critical scholarship of our own times.

Nevertheless, even earlier centuries had an awareness of the special qualities of Matthew's Gospel. In the history of the Church there constantly arose focal points in the reception of Matthew – that is, situations and movements during which his Gospel was read with special care and understood particularly well. This can be seen with special clarity in the historical reception of the Sermon on the Mount: medieval monasticism was, beyond a doubt, one of the areas where Matthew's 'Gospel of Jesus' Commandments' was central. The same can also be said of marginal movements of the Reformation. Whereas Luther, to take but one example, viewed John rather than Matthew as the most important of the Gospels, the Gospel of Matthew was central to the Anabaptists. It did not require any special theological training in order to be understood; Jesus' commandments and the stories about him speak for themselves. What is necessary for an understanding of Matthew's Gospel is, as we have seen, obedience, for only he who brings forth fruit will, in the end, understand what Jesus is saying to him.[15] For this reason Matthew's Gospel has always,

---

[15] See pp. 85–91 above.

and in a quite special way, been a book for ordinary men and women, not for theologians and sages.

MATTHEW AND CHRISTIANS TODAY

To understand Matthew's Gospel today means doing exactly as Matthew did long ago with his own Christ tradition. It means rethinking his Gospel in light of our own experience of history and of current events; it means retelling the story of Jesus, the 'God with us', with Matthew's help and reinterpreting the 'gospel of the kingdom' anew for today. But what forms might this take? What aspects of Matthew's story and his interpretation of Jesus' preaching are so important that we would wish to linger with him? Where must we change his story of Jesus?

Let me begin with the negative side. The conflict between Jesus and Judaism should no longer be taken as the core of Matthew's story. We know that Jesus was not put to death by 'the Jews' as a whole. He was a Jew, and was sent by God to redeem Israel. The story of the first-century breach between Jesus' adherents and the nation of Israel was a tragedy unforeseen by Jesus himself and in many respects entirely fortuitous. Perhaps it might have been avoided altogether under different historical circumstances, without the appearance of Paul, say, or without the tensions resulting from the Jewish War. From Jesus' standpoint it is conceivable that the Gentile Mission and the separation from the Law might never have come about – the very events to which we owe the existence of our own Church, and which made Israel's affirmation of Jesus all the more difficult. Such historical coincidences of far-reaching import oblige us to exercise humility. Moreover, we Gentile Christians of today have not suffered persecution at the hands of Jews and need not come to grips with such experiences. On the contrary, over the centuries the Church has figured among the persecutors of Israel. Today it is in a position to reflect theologically on such positive encounters with Jews that were nevertheless made possible, particularly in this century, in spite of the Holocaust. Our story of Jesus, in other words, should express gratitude toward Judaism rather than bitterness. We must also consider the terrible consequences resulting for Jews from, for example, Matthew's Israel theology or from other books of the Bible and their Christian interpretation. These are the experiences that *we* must come to grips with – and they are quite different from Matthew's. On this point, then, our story of Jesus, the 'God with us', will have to take on an entirely different hue from the Matthean story.[16]

But much of our understanding could be the same as Matthew's. The experiences he gathered within his tiny minority community on its path to righteousness can serve as a corrective in the mass churches of today, especially the western, Protestant denominations with their superabundance of doctrine. By giving precedence to grace over ethics, to confession of faith over community, these churches have become virtually indistinguishable from secular society. In many respects Matthew poses a greater challenge to us than do Paul or John for the simple reason that he is the more remote from us today.

Matthew is a theologian beholden to experience. Like Matthew's, our story of Jesus, the 'God with us', must mirror concrete and tangible experiences with Christ. 'God is with us', after all, implies that something is taking place in our lives! In the churches of today, now grown vague and inchoate, *our* story of Jesus should, like Matthew's, make clear that salvation has something to do with healing, faith with conduct, prayer with miracles, and sacrament with feeding. Grace is concrete and non-metaphorical. Matthew points out just how important and concrete is the forgiveness of sins, far more concrete than mere knowledge of a merciful God. Experiences with Christ must not be allowed to devolve into general propositions. Thus, Matthew is intent on recounting a Jesus narra-

---

[16] It is not enough tacitly to repress the anti-Jewish passages in Matthew and elsewhere in the Bible. Rather, the point is explicitly to kindle a new and critical understanding of the biblical canon by deliberately grappling with these passages, thereby precluding new forms of anti-Jewish misreadings of the New Testament in the future.

tive whose principal object is the experience of stories, not the learning of rules. It is for this very reason that he subordinates Jesus' doctrine to his Jesus story rather than vice versa. Stories convey experiences; stories allow us to partake of experiences; stories preclude abstraction.

Especially significant in Matthew's story of Jesus is the experience of prayer. That the core of the Sermon on the Mount is found in prayer – i.e that the Lord's Prayer is not located somewhere else in the Bible – is of cardinal importance to Matthew. The imitation of Jesus' way, then, means action *and* prayer, daring *and* prayer, obedience *and* prayer, suffering *and* prayer. This 'and' is central to Matthew's cast of thought. To him, faith, action and suffering are all conducted in and accompanied by prayer. Conversely, prayer is always connected with daring, obedience, activity and suffering. This is the truth enacted and taught by the Matthean Jesus.

Today our story of Jesus, the Immanuel, must make plain to our theory-bound churches that to be a church is to experience community. A church is a community of doers, not merely of listeners of the Word (a church of listeners does not require a community!). This community does not permit distinctions between greater and lesser members, or between teachers and non-teachers. Matthew makes clear that the predominance of theologians in the Church is a dubious state of affairs, given that all that ultimately matters are the fruits of our actions.

To my way of thinking, Matthew can still teach us just how important are models and exemplars for the conduct of our lives. Jesus, the subject of Matthew's story, is a model for the life of the community. He is not simply a guide whose good deeds are deserving of imitation by others. Those who speak of Jesus as a 'mere' guide understand next to nothing of the force such a guide can exert! Guides inspire us and impart courage. Matthew depicts Jesus as a human being whose deeds and words are in perfect concord with each other (as was doubtless the case with the real Jesus!). In our age, when the Word has suffered an inflation of meanings, this point deserves to be stressed: Matthew depicts Jesus as a man of deeds, not of words only.

But Matthew also shows us where obedience to the will of the Father eventually leads: to persecution, suffering and death. He depicts how, precisely in his death, God himself takes matters in hand and thwarts human actions. In this respect, Matthew's story of Jesus is a story of hope for the persecuted and afflicted. It is more than the story of a model: it is the story of God's promise. The very one who serves us as an exemplar through his obedience is also God's presence in our midst. Matthew's story of Jesus is a story of God.[17] He has given us a highly concrete story of God's presence in the midst of life. For men and women of today, who have ready access to other people and other role models, but not to God, it is important to assert that Matthew's concrete story of Jesus was nothing less than an attempt to speak of God. Any contemporary story of Jesus must speak of God as Matthew did. Otherwise, the story will fade away into nothingness, like many another good story.

---

[17] Cf. the 'horizontal' and 'vertical' dimensions of Matthew's Son of God theology, discussed on pp. 97ff.

Further reading

EXTENSIVE COMMENTARIES

Davies, W. D., and Allison, D. C., *A Critical and Exegetical Commentary on the Gospel according to St. Matthew*, ICC, 1–2 (Edinburgh: Clark, 1987–91).
Excellent, with many detailed philological and historical observations.

Gnilka, J., *Das Matthäusevangelium*, HThK, i/1–2 (Freiburg, Basle and Vienna: Herder, 1986–88).
Readable and reasonable.

Gundry, R. H., *Matthew: a Commentary on his Literary and Theological Art* (Grand Rapids: Eerdmans, 1982).
With emphasis on redaction criticism.

Luz, U., *Matthew 1–7: a Commentary*, trans. W. Linss (Edinburgh: T & T Clark, 1990).
With an emphasis on the history of interpretation. Volume 2, on Matthew 8–17, appeared in German in 1990; volume 3, on Matthew 18–25, is scheduled for publication in 1995. The American edition of volume 2 (Matthew 8–20) will appear in the *Hermeneia* series in 1995.

SHORT COMMENTARIES

France, R. T., *The Gospel according to St. Matthew*, TNTC, 1 (Grand Rapids: Eerdmans, 1985).
Informative and usefully critical on several 'self-evident assumptions of scholarly research'.

Meier, J. P., *Matthew* (Wilmington: Glazier, 1981²).
Very useful, with emphasis on redaction criticism.

Schnackenburg, R., *Das Matthäusevangelium*, NEB, 1/1–2 (Würzburg: Echter, 1985–87).
Brilliant short commentary, centred on redaction criticism.

Schweizer, E., *The Good News according to Matthew* (Atlanta: John Knox, 1975).
Already twenty years old but not outdated, thanks to its wealth of material and theological insight.

IMPORTANT MONOGRAPHS

Bornkamm, G., Barth, G. and Held, H. J., *Tradition and Interpretation in Matthew* (Philadelphia: Westminster, 1963).
A Matthean 'classic' in redaction criticism.
Frankemölle, H., *Jahwebund und Kirche Christi*, *NTA.NF*, 10 (Münster: Aschendorf, 1974).
Important particularly for the discovery of the 'Immanuel' Christology.
Guelich, R. A., *The Sermon on the Mount: a Foundation for Understanding* (Waco: Word, 1982).
Most important exegetical monograph on Matthew 5–7 in English.
Howell, D., *Matthew's Inclusive Story: a Study in the Narrative Rhetoric of the First Gospel*, *JSNT.S*, 42 (Sheffield: ISOT Press, 1990).
Narrative–critical study with good reflections on the implied reader of Matthew.
Kingsbury, J. D., *Matthew as Story* (Philadelphia: Fortress, 1986).
Reconstructs the 'plot' of Matthew.
Marguerat, D., *Le jugement dans l'Evangile de Matthieu* (Geneva: Éditions Labor et Fides, 1981).
Excellent monograph on the Last Judgement in Matthew.
Overman, J. A., *Matthew's Gospel and Formative Judaism: the Social World of the Matthean Community* (Minneapolis: Augsburg Fortress, 1990).
Excellent study on the historical and sociological background of Matthew.
Schweizer, E., *Matthäus und seine Gemeinde*, *SBS*. 71 (Stuttgart: Katholisches Bibelwerk, 1974).
Companion to his commentary, containing important papers.
Stanton, G., *A Gospel for a New People* (Edinburgh: T & T Clark, 1992).
Excellent collection of papers on Matthew, particularly valuable for its discussion of Matthew's relation to Judaism.
Strecker, G., *Der Weg der Gerichtigkeit: Untersuchungen zur Theologie des Matthäus*, *FRLANT*, 82 (Göttingen: Vandenhoeck & Ruprecht, 1962).

Another 'classic' of redaction criticism which has long awaited an English translation.

Trilling, W., *Das wahre Israel: Studien zur Theologie des Matthäusevangeliums* (Leipzig: St Benno, 1975³).

Redaction–critical monograph, important for its discussion of Matthew's relation with Israel.

Subject index

Index of citations from Matthew

164

28:16–20 5, 15, 37, 63, 139   28:19 12, 20
28:18 116   28:20 31, 32, 36